Crib Notes

Crib Notes

Kelly Perotti

To order additional copies of this book, contact:
Xlibris Corporation
1-888-795-4274
www.Xlibris.com
Orders@Xlibris.com
54713

Contents

Section Four: Labor and Delivery

Section Five: Life After Birth

Section Six: Settling In — A Couple Months into Mommyhood

Dedications

To my babies ~ You are my greatest joy and my biggest hope for the future. I wouldn't trade you for anything in the world (not a full night's sleep, not a bikini-ready belly). I don't remember the time before you were here, and I don't need to — it was insignificant. I love you down to the last Cheerio.

For my husband, without whom my babies would not be possible. You're the best husband who ever played along with a crazy wife, the greatest father who ever taught his boys to make "toot" noises with their mouths, and the most loyal friend — which is how this all began.

Introduction

Information Overload

It was the best of times, it was the worst of times. No, wait, that opening line is already taken. Too bad, because it is the perfect description of the times surrounding contemplating if you're ready to be a mom, getting pregnant, and having a baby. The pressure of a no-turning-back decision, the complications of conceiving, the challenges of pregnancy, and the trials of being a parent can be stressful to say the least. Despite their often-talked-about downsides, those periods of your life can also be the most rewarding.

Books that represent that combination of good and bad seemed to be lacking though. I felt that there was a void in the pregnancy and parenting section of the bookshelf. And, when I see a hole I fix it (sometimes with the correct material, sometimes with just a little clear nail polish). I found most books to either be instructional textbooks or to display women who seem to think they're too cool to be moms. I was bored by the clinical feel of the how-to's and turned off by the complaining tone of the moms who seem to regret replacing business meetings with play dates and trading their merlot for orange juice. Maybe you can relate. Although I am not pregnant now and may never be again (it's up for debate), I want there to be a resource for others who were unsatisfied with what they were finding, and were left with unanswered questions.

This is not a pregnancy or parenting book because God (along with anyone who has seen me in action) knows that I am an expert on neither. My intention was not to teach or preach but rather to inform and, hopefully, entertain. Everyone's experience is different, but a glimpse into the happenings of others during similar times can provide you with the assurance that you're in good company, or at least with some comic relief. And while the testimony that you're about to witness may not make you a better parent, it may relieve some guilt and let you know you're not alone, help you understand what the heck is going on, and laugh at the times things just seem to be falling apart.

Frank and Candid (what a beautiful couple)

I hope you'll enjoy, or at least excuse, my candor. Movies and television shows portray pregnancy and childbirth in such a quixotic way that you may be surprised to learn that pregnancy isn't all pickles and ice cream. I *love* being pregnant but it is definitely not a time for naiveté.

I wanted to know everything. I read books, I searched the web, I welcomed stories of veteran mommies (even the horrifying ones). I figured that, in this case, what I didn't know *could* hurt me. And while I knew there was no way I could predict how my experiences would be, I wanted to be aware of as many possibilities as I could. I considered knowledge as power.

While you might not want to know every last (potentially gruesome) detail, you should at least pay attention to your own body. Closing your eyes and ignoring changes may not only make you miss out on a great experience but could be potentially dangerous.

Recognizing Our Differences

Since I want you to have time to do something other than read this book during your nine month pregnancy stint, I had to make some generalizations to keep it from getting too long. While I am a heterosexual, married woman who chose to consult with an obstetrician and deliver at a hospital, I recognize and respect that not everyone fits that same profile.

While midwives assist at over two-thirds of births in European countries, they account for less than 10 percent of the births in the US. But that number has recently been on the rise. You may have chosen to have a midwife help with your delivery, or had your baby at home in your own bathtub.

Not all moms have male partners, or partners at all. Maybe you're a single mom-to-be, or your partner is neither a husband, nor a boyfriend, nor a guy at all. Advances in fertility technology and adoption laws have opened the door for more single or same sex parents than even in the recent past.

Whether your difference comes in the form of partnership or birthing method, we'll likely share some similar experiences. Please substitute 'birthing center' for 'hospital', or 'partner' for 'husband', wherever necessary. Or, ignore the specifics and focus on the big picture — enjoying what can be the most wonderful experience of your life.

Section One

Conception

have fun trying

I ran into an ex-boyfriend a few years ago and, after showing me a picture of his daughter, he told me that they were "trying for another." Later, as I drove home, all I could think was that he basically told me that lately he and his wife were having unprotected sex frequently. As I suppressed the thought that this was his attempt at bragging about his sex life, I decided never to announce that I was trying. I don't consider myself a particularly private or modest person (as you will fast figure out as you read on), but a general proclamation of intercourse to any listening party crosses the few personal boundary issues I do have. Not that people won't ask.

Chapter 1

Honeymoon Baby?
New House, New Baby?
Biological Clock Baby?

People take any chance they can to ask about, encourage, or otherwise pry into your plans to have children. And by any chance I mean weddings, moving to a new house, Arbor Day, the second Tuesday of each month . . . If you don't want to be hounded at every turn it's probably best to lay out some ground rules. If your in-laws don't think that the "Don't ask me again until our fifth anniversary" rule that you laid down at your wedding applies to them, try "Every time you mention it is another month I'm staying on birth control." Sure it may be a bluff, but the thought of delaying grandbabies will at least make them think twice before asking.

No matter what you say or how much you threaten, the fact remains that people will continue to ask periodically. I found that it was best to be prepared. And make sure your partner is on board with your response so that he doesn't reveal that you've been trying for months and that it should happen any day now while you're telling people that you want a little more time alone as a couple.

If you are trying and it's not happening for you, or just not happening as quickly as you'd like, the constant barrage of questions is a very unwanted reminder of what feels like failure. Unless they've been in that situation and remember the pain and frustration, people don't realize how hurtful their interrogation can be. I have found "We're having fun practicing" often means "Unsuccessful attempts at conception have sucked all enjoyment out of sex."

Chapter 2

Trying — Sex With Intention

When is the right time? How do you know if you're ready? Well, how did you know your partner was "the one"? How did you know when you had found the right wedding dress? It's just one of those things that you know. Maybe you have had the baby itch for a while, or maybe you just woke up one morning ready to reproduce.

From the time you make the decision to start trying, it's likely that you'll have a year before you're the proud parent of that squiggly little version of yourself. Pregnancy lasts just long enough for you to fully prepare yourself to be a mom. But even before the start of those nine months, you'll have the time it takes to get pregnant once you've started trying. This could be a matter of moments or a matter of years.

There are many different definitions of "trying". Some women chart their cycle, take their basal temperature, and monitor their mucus consistency. In case you don't remember the health talk you had in fifth grade, the average length of a menstrual cycle is 29 days. Count the first day of your period as Day 1. Ovulation usually begins around Day 14. You are most fertile during the few days surrounding ovulation. Therefore, if your cycle is regular enough to know when you ovulate, you can up your odds of getting pregnant faster. If your cycle is not consistent, then charting the length of your cycle, along with your basal temperature may help you determine when you ovulate.

Basal Body Temperature (BBT) is just a fancy name for your core body temperature. Your temperature rises slightly during ovulation. You will need to buy a special thermometer that can detect the slight differences in your temperature. It is recommended that you take your temperature each morning before you get out of bed, roughly at the same time (sounds a lot like the schedule I had to remember for the pill). If you record your temperature throughout your cycle, you will likely notice a slightly increased reading a few days mid-cycle. Since you won't know that you've ovulated until after it has already happened, you'll need to continue this for a couple months, or until you can recognize a pattern. Or, you can purchase an Ovulation Test which should indicate the 48 hours in which you should have the most success conceiving.

Those are the clean ways to determine your personal fertile time. Another method, monitoring your mucus consistency, is a much more hands-on process. Apparently your cervical mucus tells the story of your cycle. Changes in the consistency can clue you in to when you're ovulating.

The first couple days after your period, there's not much at all, if any. It's unlikely (but always possible!) that you'll get pregnant at that point. But then just before ovulation it gets thicker and sticky and may be creamy or white in consistency. Here's the fun part—when stretched between your fingers it will pull apart easily. As you get further into your cycle, you may start to notice more mucus that is likely more cloudy. At this point there is a slightly stronger possibility for conception.

The thin, stretchy, clear mucus, whose consistency is often compared to egg whites, appears at ovulation. This is when the chance for fertilization is at its highest. This is the environment that sperm like best. It's less dense than at other times, allowing the sperm to pass through to the uterus, or even live in the mucus waiting for an egg to arrive. It takes quite a determined sperm to want to hang out in mucus!

Bonus: There is a higher chance for conception if the woman has an orgasm. The increased lubrication helps the sperm travel upstream.

If you're just starting out, and aren't in any real hurry, you may just take a relaxed approach and enjoy the process. I always said, "We're not trying, but we're not *not* trying." That's when you don't renew your birth control prescription, ditch the condoms, and have sex like normal. If it happens, that's cool. If not, there's always next month.

~Chapter 3~

It *Can* Happen the First Time

In theory there are a lot of factors that need to align in order for you to get pregnant, but in reality, it seems to happen much more easily than that. Just as some women follow all the rules and still never get pregnant, others easily conceive even at times when they scientifically shouldn't be fertile. You can't always trust the science of conception.

Practice makes perfect does not necessarily apply to fertility. Having sex more frequently may increase your chance of conceiving on an odds basis, but quality counts over quantity. It may take just once to get the job done. "Meant to be" often wins out over science.

If you're child-free and/or ready and willing at the drop of a hat (or pants?), you may be having sex so often that, when you do get pregnant, it'll be difficult to determine exactly when conception took place. Because of the, ahem, level of activity within the week that conception was probable (conception is *always* possible!), there may be no way of knowing if it was actually the very first time but, my point is, it doesn't take much.

My older son is proof that you *can* get pregnant the first time you try. There are many children out there that prove that you can get pregnant without even trying — ignoring the calendar, paying no attention to position . . . and only having sex a few times in the whole month. That's how you know when it's really meant to be. Or at least that's what you tell your partner to ease the shock.

If it doesn't happen the first time — or even the first 10 times — remember that grade school mantra: if at first you don't succeed, try, try again!

~Chapter 4~

Mis-Conceptions—
Tricks to Conceiving a Boy or Girl

As if getting pregnant isn't hard enough to begin with, some couples complicate the matter by trying to conceive a specific gender. Tips, hints, and suggestions abound on the Internet. Some have medical basis while others are crazy old wives' tales (it's the tales that I'm calling crazy, not the old wives. Never call an old wife crazy . . . or old for that matter).

Landrum B. Shettles, MD is perhaps the most well-known researcher in the field of gender selection. The Shettles Method is a combination of biology and timing that can affect the sex of the baby that you conceive. Men produce two kinds of sperm, X (female) and Y (male), each with their own characteristics. X sperm are bigger and stronger, but slower. The Y sperm are smaller and weaker than their female counterparts, but are faster.

Based on those qualities, certain times of the month and positions are more favorable for conceiving one gender or the other. In order to attempt to follow these guidelines, you'll need to be pretty familiar with your cycle. So make sure you're done playing with calendars, thermometers, and mucus, before you start.

Timing is the most important component since the X and Y sperm have different life expectancies. With the egg as the target, the Y sperm are faster and tend to get there first. The X sperm are slower but can hold out longer (sounds about right). Therefore, if you're trying for a boy, you need to have sex as close as possible to ovulation so that the Y sperm has a chance to get to the egg before dying. If it's a girl you're looking for, it's recommended that you have sex three days or more before ovulation. By the time the egg is released, most of the Y sperm will have died but the X sperm will still be alive and kicking (squirming? swimming?). As you can see, this is not a large window so, without knowing exactly when you ovulate, it is easy to mix up!

The pH levels of your vagina are important as well. X (girl) sperm benefit from a more acidic environment since the acid kills off the Y (boy) sperm. Of course that means that a less acidic tract favors the conception of a boy. You're most acidic at the entrance to the vagina so depth of sexual penetration plays a part in this as well. (With all this talk of environments and entrances it feels as if we're hosting our own little biosphere down there!) The Y sperm are a little lazy (boys will be boys) and like to be dropped off right at their destination, so a position

17

that allows for deeper penetration is ideal. A more shallow penetration delivers the X sperm into their optimal, acidic, atmosphere, giving them the best chance.

Orgasms are very important for guys (duh). This apparently starts before conception even takes place. When you have an orgasm, your body releases a chemical that makes the environment more alkaline, allowing those Y sperm a better chance of survival. No orgasms allowed if you want a girl (sacrificing for your daughter already).

Finally, a high sperm count favors boys so, for a boy, refrain from sex for a few days before your predetermined target date. Not releasing for a couple days allows time for sperm build up, which sounds gross but is good in this case. Loose underwear and clothing can up sperm count so make your partner toss his tighty-whiteys if you want a son. Don't try to drop his sperm count if you're trying for a daughter though — decreased sperm count is bad for overall fertility and you may end up not conceiving at all.

Trying to control the acidity of your vagina and your partner's sperm volume can prove quite complicated and frustrating. Even if you manage to figure it all out, and do get pregnant, your odds of conceiving one sex over the other is only slightly more than the normal 50/50. Some couples who are particularly determined to control the sex of their baby turn to technology.

Sperm-sorting technology that was originally intended to prevent X-linked diseases that can only be passed to boys (medical mumbo-jumbo) is now being used to custom-design the sex of our babies. Additionally, there is a form of In Vitro fertilization that genetically screens embryos to determine their gender before implanting them in the mother. Aside from requiring perfectly fertile couples to go through the expensive and physically-taxing In Vitro fertilization process, and only increasing probability by a fraction, these procedures are ethically questionable.

Although, statistically speaking, conception is an individual event thus offering a 50/50 chance of conceiving a boy or girl each time, it seems to be true that the more children you have of one gender, the more likely you are to have another of that same sex. This tells me that pregnancy doesn't like to follow the rules. That's why I prefer to stick with the traditional methods.

In addition to technological advances and the Shettles Method detailed above, there are other ways of influencing the sex of your baby. Women who are 40 years old or older at the time of conception have a higher rate of baby girls than younger women. Girls are the result of the hormonal changes caused by severe stress as well. It is suggested that your diet can affect the gender of your children. Ditch your coffee and drink milk along with plenty of beans, nuts, and vegetables if you want a girl since higher levels of calcium and magnesium along with no caffeine seem to be a girl-friendly meal plan. Those desiring boys should choose lean meats, caffeine, and sodium (although that doesn't sound like the most well-rounded diet).

And then there are other tried and true (read: crazy) predictors. You need to ramp up your sex drive and tell your partner to back down if you want a girl—it's said that your baby will be same gender as the partner who initiated the act that led to conception. Other suggestions for conceiving a girl include putting a wooden spoon under your bed and a pink ribbon under your pillow. You can go as far with this as you'd like. Gender selection is an age old desire; French men in the Eighteenth Century believed that tying a string around their left testicle could increase their chance of producing a boy. I can't imagine that any guy wants a son that badly.

Regardless of the method you use (if any), beware—you don't want to get too picky. Just because your quick-conception earned you the nickname Fertile Myrtle the first time doesn't mean that's how it'll always be (don't worry, people are much less likely to give you a nickname when you're having trouble). Friends of mine spent close to a year working towards baby number one. So when they decided they were almost ready for another they started a few months ahead of "schedule" . . . and she was pregnant within the first week. Conversely, another couple who had conceived just two months into their first attempt, found themselves at a consultation with a fertility specialist after trying unsuccessfully to conceive again for over a year.

There are so many options. If it's just not happening for you, and you feel that you need outside help, talk to your doctor. They may be able to run some tests that give you answers. There are pharmaceutical treatments (commonly called fertility drugs) and procedures (In Vitro Fertilization, Intra-Uterine Fertilization, etc.) that you can try. Adoption is always a great alternative as well (God knows there are plenty of babies in need of a good home). These can be prohibitively expensive and not easy on you physically or emotionally but can often fulfill your desire to have a child.

This baby thing is a tricky, tricky game. It's best left in the hands of fate . . . or God, or Mother Nature, or luck, or whatever you chose to believe.

Section Two

Pregnancy

T minus 9 months

Over the next nine months your relationship with your body will change and so will your outlook on life. Your outward appearance will certainly transform. Your growing baby has a nine month lease on some prime property. You might keep your little tenant a secret for a while, but soon enough he'll make his presence well known — to you and everyone else.

The first time you feel the baby move, well, you probably won't know it. You may mistake it for hunger or a reaction to something you ate (otherwise known as gas). The poor kid is trying to say hello and you're blaming it on your lunch. Before long you'll learn to distinguish between baby movements and gastric troubles. The feeling is often described as butterflies or a fluttering. One day "Was that it?" will turn into, "Honey, feel this!" Then, at the end of your pregnancy when the baby has taken up every possible inch available, it will feel like all out assault from within!

It's not only your body that changes. Your emotions will run the gamut from fear to ecstasy, unpreparedness to impatience. It may be intimidating, or validating, that you are his sole provider; what you eat, he eats; what you breathe, he breathes. This emotional ambivalence will likely last long into parenthood.

~Chapter 1~

Taking the Test

There comes a time when you need to take a pregnancy test. Whether you've been trying, you had a contraception malfunction, you're following a hunch, or that's just what you do for fun each month, chances are that sooner or later, you'll be peeing on a stick. Just so you know, doing that without getting pee on your fingers or the floor is the first indication of your baby motor skill proficiency (more on that later).

If you've never taken a pregnancy test, let me tell you — it's the longest two minutes of your life. Whether you're keeping an eye on the clock radio on your nightstand, watching the second hand on your watch, or staring intently at a stopwatch, it will seem like it's taking longer to get the results than it did to get pregnant.

How can a little plastic pee-filled stick have that much meaning for the rest of your life? If you've been trying, or will be happy either way, it should be fun (or as fun as urinating on something can be). But it's more likely that it will be more stressful than the SATs — and harder to complete.

Depending on the type and brand, the results of the test are displayed in a number of ways. There are varying degrees of difficulty, from lines to colors and shapes. You may even have trouble deciphering the results of the one that makes the word PREGNANT magically appear on the screen. And I hope you splurged and bought the twin pack because, no matter what the results, you won't believe it the first time.

~Chapter 2~

Sharing the Good News

So you're pregnant, now what? You're probably so excited that you want to shout it from the rooftop. But be careful, you're in no condition to be on a ladder.

Some people spread the good news when their period's a day late. I prefer to wait until Week 11 or 12 when it's confirmed, I've heard a heartbeat, and I know there's a good viability rate. This is completely a 'to each her own' kind of thing; there is no right or wrong timing.

Regardless of your preference, your partner will probably be the first person you tell—although not always. I've heard stories of women who hatch an elaborate plan that involves many people knowing before her partner even has a clue.

Or perhaps your partner battled you for the best view of the test and found out the same instant as you so breaking the news isn't an issue. Either way, after possibly spending the previous ten years trying *not* to get a girl pregnant, a guy is finally able to feel a sense of accomplishment. There's a certain pride in knowing you have good swimmers and there's no better indicator than impregnating a woman. Even if you believe it had more to do with your ocean than his swimmers, let it go. This is a victory you can let him have.

If you decide to wait a few weeks or months before telling everyone you're pregnant, you'll have to work on your poker face. Once it's on your mind everything you see, hear, or talk about seems to be related to having a baby. You'll have to act normal when you hear your best friend's sister-in-law is pregnant. You'll have to eat your lunch silently while your co-worker (the one without children) talks about the dangers of eating tuna during pregnancy (even though, having read multiple studies on the topic, you're the clear expert). You'll have to try not to smirk when you're shopping with a friend and ask, "Does this dress make me look pregnant?" And then you'll have to lie when she says, "No. Why? Are you?!"

When you do tell everyone, you should anticipate a mixed bag of reactions. Someone will say she knew all along. She'll give you a list of reasons how she figured it out, probably none of which are true. Be ready to hear that people have been thinking you looked fat lately. Expect at least one person to be underwhelmed. Jealousy from a friend who's been trying, worry from your mom that you're not quite ready, indifference from that catty girl at work . . . some reactions will be better than others but none should take any excitement away from you.

If you're working when you get pregnant you'll eventually need to tell your boss. When you tell her is your choice but will probably be largely dependant on your relationship, how quickly you start to show, and your post-baby work plan. It's best to have a plan, not to just run into her office yelling and crying with joy.

Familiarize yourself with your state's family and maternity leave laws (more on that later), as well as your company's policies. If you're planning to stay at work for the duration of your pregnancy, assure your boss that you'll try to schedule as many doctor's appointments as possible outside of work time. And make sure your IT guy isn't monitoring your Internet usage because no matter how strong a work ethic you have, you *will* be reading up on fetal development ("This week your baby is the size of a strawberry."), and searching for baby names (Is Jacob too common? Is Gage too weird?).

~Chapter 3~

"Morning" Sickness and Meal Plans

As anyone who has ever experienced it will tell you, morning sickness is quite a misnomer. The symptoms often last all day long, sometimes increasing as the day goes on, with hunger and fatigue being fierce aggravators.

With your stomach churning, your head aching, and your gag reflex exaggerated, it may take nothing more than a whiff of someone's lunch to put you over the edge. Just like your cup size and the number of times a day you pee, your sense of smell is increased. The smell of the mango air freshener, the one that smells nothing like mangoes but is a perfectly pleasant fragrance, may now make your eyes water with disgust; the aftershave of the guy in the next office, which sneaks under your door in a green noxious fog reminiscent of early horror flicks, may be vomit-inducing. Like all pregnancy symptoms, this too will soon be gone.

It seems cruel that when you're sick and the breadth of your diet will start at saltines and end at dry toast, nutrition is needed now more than possibly ever. As long as you're eating something, you and the baby will be ok. You should be taking prenatal vitamins, or a doctor-approved multi-vitamin. These supplements will fill in the nutritional gaps for the few weeks that your taste buds are out of whack.

Before getting pregnant I ate relatively healthful foods. I kept my meals nutritious and well balanced and indulged my sweet tooth with snacks. But once morning sickness kicked in, it was crackers or dry cereal in bed, and whatever I could stomach for the rest of the day. Yogurt, salad, chicken, and most fruits and vegetables — normally my staples — were nausea-inducing. Soft pretzels, bagels, crackers, and popcorn filled in my otherwise empty diet.

But girl cannot live on carbs alone (sad but true). Luckily, as the morning sickness passed with my first trimester, so did the health food aversions. Fruit, meat and vegetables were soon incorporated back into my meal plan. A banana now accompanied the English muffin, and chicken filled part of my pasta dish. (Strangely, feeling so sick had been reassuring to me. My nausea was replaced with anxiety when I suddenly started to feel better!)

If you're one of the lucky few who skips the morning sickness and feels great from day one to delivery, maybe you're experiencing cravings. Some say that cravings are your body's way of telling you what you need. A desire for pickles and ice cream may mean you need sodium and calcium. Others say this is a bogus theory and that it's the taste—not the nutritional components—that you want. Either way, my grandmother says you have to give the baby what it wants. And when else is it more universally-acceptable to eat an ice cream sundae for breakfast?

Grandmotherly advice aside, my doctor told me that there are a few cravings that are not ok to indulge. If, during your pregnancy, you have a hankering for dirt or metal it could be a sign of an iron deficiency. The name for this unusual desire for non-edible items—laundry detergent and dirt are among the more bizarre, ice is a more tame choice—is pica. Since none of the items most commonly chosen have a real high iron count, this is a pretty inexplicable craving. I say pregnant or not, *anytime* you have taste for dirt you should alert a doctor!

There's an old adage about eating for two. While it is very important that you increase your food intake, preferably with healthful foods, it's not necessary to double up. Adding nutritious snacks and moderately increasing your portion size should be sufficient. Your doctor will monitor your weight and the size of the baby. Don't stress over the numbers on the scale or the size of your maternity jeans. But do remember—You are more than entitled to extra comfort foods and, of course, to satisfy your cravings, but unless you're looking forward to keeping extra pounds after the baby's born, don't use pregnancy as an excuse for every day to be a free for all.

Chapter 4

Weighing Your Options—
The Importance of Gaining Weight

There is no absolute number when it comes to the amount of weight you should gain. A common range is 25-35 pounds, but your goal should be determined by you and your doctor based on your pre-pregnancy weight and health level. Pregnancy is not the time to diet. Nutrition is very important, so adding lean proteins, good fats, and plenty of fruits and veggies is a great way to up your calories.

If you experience the strain of morning sickness that includes puking on an hourly basis, you may actually drop weight before you start to gain it back. If you're carrying a little extra weight to begin with you might not notice weight gain right away. (Some say that the baby steals from your supply!) Some women gain a bunch of weight at the beginning (consider this front loading), others only gain a few pounds then make up for it at the end (call it making up for lost time). Don't worry about how much you're gaining or not gaining—it'll all even out by the end.

I had two completely different pregnancies, yet gained almost the exact amount of weight each time. A doctor in my practice once told me to aim high and not to worry because I'd lose two-thirds of the weight quickly after the baby was born. It was a skinny male doctor. I didn't believe him. No personal experience, no real point of reference, no credibility.

He was right.

No matter what, you're *going* to gain weight. You *need* to gain weight. The baby needs to grow and you need to be able to sustain your life and another. At an ultrasound towards the end of my pregnancy, they estimated that the baby was about 7 pounds. I had gained 28 by that point. What the hell were the other 21 pounds made up of?!

This is an average of how it all adds up:

   Amniotic fluid = 2 pounds
   Baby = 7-8 pounds
   Maternal blood = 4 pounds
   Maternal breast tissue = 2 pounds
   Maternal fat and nutrient stores = 7 pounds
   Maternal tissue fluids= 4 pounds
   Placenta = 1-2 pounds
   Uterus = 2 pounds

Based on the average weights above, you effortlessly lose 18 pounds within just weeks of delivery (baby and placenta are out, fluids begin to normalize). Seems a little idealistic, I know. Remember that your body is smart. It's going to hold on to what it needs. But that's months away. For now, just focus on how to hide a belly that you can't suck in.

~Chapter 5~

Wardrobe Malfunctions

Thankfully, clothing designers finally realized that some women like to maintain some sense of style during pregnancy. In the past, many pregnant women looked like they were wearing a tent. Now, although I noticed a pretty drastic increase in decorative ribbons and bows compared to my normal attire, it's not too difficult to find cool maternity clothes. And at a time when it looks like you packed on 10 pounds when you really only gained 4, clothes can make all the difference.

Before you resort to wearing crushed velvet baby doll tops and shapeless trousers, check out your favorite stores. There are so many designers making maternity clothes. Some only sell their maternity lines on the Internet, while others have adapted their stores to include racks—or even whole departments—of maternity clothes. I was thrilled to find *normal* clothes that were just slightly modified to fit my huge belly. Many popular companies have expanded their brands to include maternity clothes—and quite an assortment at that.

There's a wide range of styles and shapes. Some shirts are fitted and show off your belly, some just accent it with empire waists or a swingy shape. Some pants have full over-your-belly bands, others have just a few inches of banded elastic for stretch-ability and support, still others have normal button and zipper waistbands.

No matter what style you choose, you will immediately notice that maternity pants are *so* comfortable. You'll be wondering why you waited so long to wear them and you won't want to take them off.

~Chapter 6~

Sex with Obstacles

Next time you feel like having sex, put a basketball between you and your partner and try to make everything match up. You'll then have some idea of what it's like to have sex while you're pregnant. Books advise trying different positions but they're all pretty awkward. Even if you do manage to manipulate your recently-enlarged body into some creative position, there's something really unromantic about needing pillow props and support systems to make love.

The mechanics may be the least of your worries though. Hormonal changes caused by pregnancy can quickly send your sex drive south. No double entendre there—I literally mean you won't want to have sex. Aside from the physical facts that you've gained 14 pounds in two months, you're off your skin medication (adult acne is a cruel joke), and you're completely exhausted from vomiting the whole day, the desire just isn't there. God knows you have plenty of emotions these days, but horniness may not be one of them.

But that's not the case for everyone. Some women report an increased desire for sex. It's most common that once you recover from the negative side effects of the first trimester and start to feel more like a human again, your sex drive will bounce back. Since your libido is largely controlled by levels of estrogen and progesterone, which fluctuate throughout your pregnancy, by the start of your second trimester you may find yourself more interested in sex than you've been for months.

The satisfaction of making a baby and the anticipation of being parents may have brought you and your partner closer. This feeling of increased intimacy might be just the boost you need to revive your sex life. Plus, since you're already pregnant you can enjoy making love without the hassle of dealing with contraceptives.

Due to the increased hormone levels along with extra blood flow to your pelvic area, some studies show that orgasms can be more intense and easier to achieve while you're pregnant, especially during your second trimester. That may be the best news you heard since you found out you were pregnant—and give you something to look forward to!

Here's a fun fact for you—your uterus actually hardens when you have an orgasm. It happens every time (the hardening, not the orgasm, sadly), but since your uterus is so much bigger and protrudes from your abdomen, it's much easier to tell. You know what that means ladies—there's no faking it now! The gig is up, your cover is blown . . . so to speak.

31

Not many things about pregnancy disgusted me (and there are some pretty nasty things) but that grossed me out. That, and when the baby all of a sudden started moving around in the middle of doing it. It seemed to tie pregnancy and sex together and, although I know that's virtually the closest cause and effect relationship there is, I don't like to think about the baby while I'm having sex.

~Chapter 7~

Sleeping (or not)

Despite being so tired, you may find yourself having trouble sleeping. Whether physical (you get up to pee, again, and can't fall back asleep due to aching hips), or psychological (how much is delivery really going to hurt?) it sucks to be wide awake when you just want to sleep. Just consider it training. You're naturally preparing yourself for being up with the baby several times a night.

Trying New Positions in the Bedroom

It's recommended that you sleep on your side (left is best) but if you're a belly sleeper you may have some serious adjusting to do. If you prefer to sleep on your side or your back that may be out of the question after about your first trimester since the weight of the baby makes it hard to breathe. That heavy or numb feeling indicates that you're getting decreased amounts of oxygen and blood flow, not only to you but to the baby as well.

Looks like you'll be forced to learn to fall asleep on your side. I adapted quickly but soon my hips were sore from the pressure caused by my ever-growing belly. I tried propping a pillow under my belly and between my legs but that felt awkward and made it hard to move. And rolling over was a near impossible feat. I needed to switch sides and give each hip a break so repositioning every so often was necessary. It was sometimes easier and less painful to sit up, turn around, and then lay back down, than it was to roll over. Between choreographing the movement and rebuilding my support system of pillows, sleeping had never been so complicated.

Dancing in the Sheets

You've probably heard of Restless Leg Syndrome (RLS) — sometimes a tingly or jumpy sensation, or literally the feeling that you can't keep your legs still. The symptoms usually go away if you walk around or shake your legs, but the relief only lasts while you're moving and, as you can't sleep while you're moving, that can mean no sleep once again.

Up to a quarter of all pregnant women report experiencing RLS during their pregnancy (vitamin deficiencies, medications such as antihistamines or antidepressants, and ingesting too much caffeine or alcohol are just a few of the other possible causes) but luckily, it usually goes away on its own after giving birth.

As someone who occasionally experiences this while not pregnant, I was definitely affected while I was pregnant. Not only were my legs jumpy but my arms would feel that way too. I would sit up in bed and shake my arms like some music conductor on speed. After delivery I thought it went away, until one night I was nursing the baby and my arm jumped like I was a marionette. There wasn't much I could do without disrupting my son so I just kept shaking my hand like some crazy jive dancer and it eventually stopped. I know that's a lot of analogies but it makes you feel pretty animated—and is more annoying than all three of them put together.

To Pee or Not to Pee, There is No Question

While you're up walking the extra energy out of your legs, you might as well stop by the bathroom. If you don't have to pee now you will soon. If there is one flaw in the layout of a woman's body it is that the bladder lies directly under the uterus that houses your squirming, kicking baby. The pressure caused by your ever-expanding belly is enough to send you running (read: waddling) to the nearest toilet. And a kick from your little darling may just cause a moment of panic while you wonder if the kegels you've been doing have made you strong enough to keep it from trickling out.

Kegel exercises are done by contracting the muscles of your pelvic floor. If you're not sure how to do them, try stopping yourself from peeing mid-stream and you'll immediately know what I'm talking about. By repeating this contraction, you're conditioning the muscles and preparing them for the trauma they are about to endure. Uh, I mean, strengthening them which may lead to a faster delivery, less chance of a tear or episiotomy, and decreased probability of post-partum incontinence.

I did my kegels. I did not push for very long with either birth, and thankfully didn't suffer from incontinence, but I did have an episiotomy both times. So, you can weigh your options. I *can* say that you don't have much of an excuse as this is the most discrete, least strenuous form of exercise that exists. It requires no monthly membership and you already have all the equipment needed. And if something that you can do while sitting at a red light could keep you from peeing your pants in a couple months, why not give it a shot?

~Chapter 8~

Side Effects May Include . . .

We often see commercials for new drugs that spend the majority of their air time listing the side effects. I always thought that the primary problem must be pretty bad if you'd be willing to chance all those possible complications. Then I started to think about the "side effects" of pregnancy — those symptoms that occur in many cases, but seem to have little to do with actually having a baby.

If, before you conceived, you had read the following disclaimer, would you have proceeded as you did?

Caution: Pregnancy may cause carpal tunnel syndrome, a desire to eat dirt, gum disease, mood swings, increased hair growth followed by considerable hair loss, heartburn, swelling of the limbs, rashes . . . the list goes on and on!

How the heck does being pregnant cause carpal tunnel syndrome? I thought that was caused by being on the computer too much. What do my wrists have to do with having a baby? This one can be blamed on fluid retention causing pressure on the nerve that's found in the narrow space between your wrist bones and the ligament that runs along the side of your arm.

When my Crest started turning pink I thought maybe it meant I was having a girl but then I did a little research. Apparently the increase in hormones causes your gums to react even more aversely to plaque than normal. Add in the extra blood volume and you have bleeding gums. Great.

One thing I managed to avoid was PUPPS. This insanely itchy rash usually begins on your pregnant belly and then spreads to your hands, feet, sides of your legs, and wherever else it wants to, depending on the severity. There's no real known reason for PUPPS. It seems somewhat related to the stretching of skin. There is no treatment other than oatmeal baths and compresses but it usually disappears within a week of giving birth.

Perhaps the strangest thing that I experienced was not an affliction but rather an aversion. I had a strong repugnance for water. Drinking it was repulsive; bathing in it was disgusting. A warm shower is usually a place of relaxing solitude but I dreaded it each day (and admittedly skipped it sometimes). Explain the biological reason behind that one. Anyone? Anyone?

It's funny how when you read about most symptoms they are usually preceded by the word "moderate". I would estimate that the heartburn that I experienced was much closer to dragon-like than moderate. Who are they kidding? Even though most of these "side effects" are categorized as normal, you should talk to your doctor about how they are affecting you and your pregnancy.

Section Three

Preparing for Baby

Ready or not, here it comes

No amount of books or classes can truly prepare you for parenthood. It's one of those things that you have to learn as you go. Sure, upfront information and pointers along the way can be helpful, but ultimately, it's an on-going learning experience. The sooner you stop trying to control everything, and instead introduce a little flexibility into your day, the sooner you'll find success . . . and that's coming from a control freak, so you should believe me.

Chapter 1

All You Ever Wanted to Know (and then some) — Prenatal Class

A birthing class may help you understand what will happen behind those delivery room doors. Classes are offered by most hospitals and are also held by outside organizations and groups. Schedules can be a one-day crash course or several weeks in length. It is recommended that you take the class sometime in the beginning of your third trimester so that you are near enough to the end of your pregnancy to remember everything that you learn, but far enough from your due date that if the baby makes an unexpected early appearance you'll be prepared.

Be ready for the X-rated video. Many classes show videos of both a vaginal birth and a C-section delivery. The video will likely look outdated and star a woman at the height of labor. Try not to be frightened by her reaction to pain or distracted by her need to wax. The intention of the video is to illustrate the progress of labor and birth.

You'll learn about the signs of true labor. Your instructor will teach you how to assess pain, how to tell if your water broke, and how to count contractions. You need to be familiar with these signs as they indicate that true labor has begun or is soon to come. The level of pain, frequency of contractions, and status of your water sack are also the things you'll need to tell your doctor when you call. Don't be surprised if they tell you to hang out at home a little longer, or bring you to the hospital only to then send you home until you make more progress.

Perhaps the biggest reason women attend prenatal classes is to learn about their pain management options. The classes can provide you with the information that you need in order to make decisions about your desired birthing method. Although classes focusing on a specific method are available, most classes will provide an overview of several techniques.

Birthing Methods and Pain Management

Contrary to popular belief, Lamaze is a birthing method, not the general term for coping with labor. Lamaze is often misconstrued as an all natural method, as it focuses on breathing patterns, partner support, and a birth free of medical intervention, but it actually does not rule out medication for pain relief. The true intention of Lamaze is to fully inform women so that they can make educated decisions as to the details of their delivery.

The Bradley Method takes a harder stand against pain medication's place in the delivery room — basically that it has none. This method teaches total relaxation, not through specific breathing patterns, but rather total immersion and involvement in delivery. A woman, along with her partner, should focus *on* the labor as opposed to the distracting take-your-mind-off-of-it methods suggested by others.

These are just two of many birthing methods. Massage, movement, and water therapy are alternative coping mechanisms. And then there are drugs. The most commonly known, and most commonly requested pain treatment is the epidural. This is a type of regional anesthesia, meaning that it blocks pain to a certain area (you know which area I mean in this case). It is meant to numb the pain but, depending on your body's sensitivity and the administered dose, you may not be able to feel your toes, much less contractions. For others, you may still feel dull contractions that are more annoying than painful. This level of awareness may help you in the long run; knowing when you're having a contraction can help you push more effectively.

Many women fear that their epidural may run out or wear off before the baby is born. However, epidurals are administered through a catheter, delivering a continuous flow of medication. Your anesthesiologist, OB, or nurse can monitor your progress and adjust the flow as necessary. Some downsides of having an epidural is that, once the catheter is inserted, you are not allowed out of bed. Also, it may weaken your contractions, potentially slowing your progress and delaying delivery. Chances are you won't mind the extra hour of relaxation — it may be the last you get for a while.

Other somewhat lesser medication options are found in the form of narcotics. Instead of blocking pain, these intravenous (IV) drugs are often said to "take the edge off". By relieving some of the pain and helping you relax, you may be able to cope more easily and focus on your other techniques such as visualization and breathing. Depending on how your body reacts, you may become sleepy or feel out of sorts. Some women find it irritating to have a foggy head or feel out of control. This is not always a stand-alone option; if the pain relief is not sufficient for you, you can still request an epidural.

Many classes also cover newborn care — information about what to expect during your little one's first few weeks of life outside the womb. You'll learn what the first few diaper changes will look like (otherwise you may be shocked), how to give him his first bath, how to care for the umbilical cord/belly button, and similar firsts. An overview of breastfeeding may be taught as well. Usually in depth classes and seminars that teach such things as holding positions and correct latch are offered separately.

Prenatal classes are a great opportunity to meet other expectant parents — at which point you may comment to your partner how small you are compared to all the other huge mamas in the class (just keep telling yourself that . . .). The overall goal of the class is for you to learn enough to calm your fears, and make informed decisions regarding all of the aspects of labor and delivery.

~Chapter 2~

Best Laid Plans

All pregnant women wonder what labor and delivery will be like, and may even have specific ideas in mind for the way they'd like it to play out. Even if you just want to go with the flow and take things as they come, you'll likely want to give some thought to some of the details of your baby's birth. Some women choose to take those thoughts one step up by creating a birth plan.

Exploring your options gives you an opportunity to think about how you'd like your baby's birth to be handled. It may help to review your plans with your partner and your doctor. Let's assume that a discussion with your partner is sufficient; your doctor, however, may not recall all the details of your personal agenda. Since you won't likely be up for the extended conversation at that moment, consider filing your birth plan with your doctor. A copy can be included in your medical chart and referenced when the time comes.

Although there's no way to dictate every part of such an unpredictable event, a birth plan usually includes your preferences regarding birthing location, allowing others to be present, induction, epidural or other pain management, cesarean delivery, episiotomy, and can even extend to post-delivery details such as breastfeeding and circumcision. This is just a short list of some of the things you may consider.

Whether you choose to document and circulate a birth plan or not, you'll need to allow for change. Even if you have specific ideas concerning every aspect of your baby's birth, it is important to stay flexible. It's likely that, even during a delivery without complications, you'll have to stray from your plan. Try to remember that the health and well-being of you and the baby are the main priority. Do not be disappointed if your natural birth turns into a C-section, or you willingly collapse into bed instead of walking your way to 10 centimeters.

~Chapter 3~

Visits to the Doctor

Depending on your risk level and the visit schedule of your doctor, you'll most likely start out with monthly appointments and eventually go once a week for the last couple weeks. These appointments are a chance to hear the baby's heartbeat, ask about whatever weird symptom has popped up since your last visit, and overall reassure you that everything is ok.

The first appointment is pretty standard. There's likely to be a lot of talking but not much examining. Be prepared — they'll want to know some family history as well as the date of the first day of your last period. That's what they use to calculate your due date. They may ask you the date of conception but, whether you swear you know the moment it happened, "Monday the 6th at 8:46pm", or your closest guess is, "Uh, June?", they'll likely trust the 'date of last period' calculation until your ultrasound or growth pattern tells them otherwise.

By the end of those nine months it feels like you're in that office all the time. You have more face time with your doctor than with your partner and your doctor definitely sees you naked more often than your partner does. The receptionists and nurses not only know your name but know the list of names you're working on for the baby. By your last scheduled appointment before your due date, with a mere glance at your fully-clothed body they can say, "Oh you dropped!" or "See ya' next week — that baby's not ready." I took comfort in their interest; I felt I was in good hands . . . literally.

It's important to feel comfortable with the employees at your practice. It's hard not to build up a friendly report with someone you hand your first-morning urine to once a month. You don't have to become BFFs with a nurse or invite your doctor to yoga, you just have to be comfortable enough to ask questions or report issues — and use the word vagina frequently without giggling. (Any term of endearment that you have for your vagina must be abandoned until you give birth — or at least restricted to the privacy of home.)

You can only trust the Internet to a certain extent, and pregnancy is not the time to risk it. If you don't know what something means, just ask. Most of the words cannot be figured out using derivative or context clues. I have a degree in English and I thought "effaced" had something to do with which direction the baby was facing. It actually refers to the shortening and thinning of your cervix as it prepares itself for the baby to pass through. Hey! It's not nice to laugh at other people's mistakes.

A lot of the pregnancy-related terms you read or hear about are misleading, and misunderstood by those who have never been pregnant. A friend of mine (really a friend, not a cover up for another one of my own misconceptions) thought that your vagina dilated. I hope you know that's wrong. Your cervix is what dilates (it's really all about the cervix, isn't it?). The opening of your cervix widens, usually to about 10 centimeters, to allow the baby to pass into your vaginal canal. Your vaginal opening stays its normal size until the baby begins to crown.

~Chapter 4~

Seeing is Believing

At some point you'll likely have an ultrasound. This is otherwise known as a bladder endurance test. The instructions might as well read: Drink 48 ounces of water then sit in a waiting room for forty-five minutes while a baby uses your bladder as a trampoline. An ultrasound tech once said that my bladder was *too* full and promptly instructed me to let a little bit out. Impossible. I had been holding it so long that it took a minute for me to start but once I did I was so distracted by the sweet feeling of relief that it took a while to stop. I was so scared that they'd make me come back another day and start all over.

Once you're finally called, the technician will take a million measurements and then attempt to point out the baby's body parts and internal organs on a small black and white screen. If you can't get a perspective on the baby—and most people can't—just ask the tech to explain and point it out again. And don't worry, in a few more months your baby will likely bear a stronger resemblance to you than to Skeletor as it does now. Just take your little photos and show them to everyone you know. Be sure to make fun of them when they can't tell what's what in the picture.

The hardest decision after deciding *when* to have a baby is deciding whether or not to try to find out the sex of the baby. If you don't want to know (my own personal recommendation), be sure to make that abundantly clear to the ultrasound tech. Even after saying I didn't want to know and even looking away while she scanned over any area that could give it away, she said, "I could tell you if you wanted." Great. Did that mean there was a clear penis shot and that it was obviously a boy? I guess it could just as easily have been the lack of a penis that tipped her off as to the baby's sex, but I couldn't help but feel that she gave it away after knowing I didn't want to find out.

Then there were *all* the guesses. Family members, friends, random people in the grocery store, everyone had a guess. I was carrying low, it must be a boy; I was eating chocolate, it must be a girl . . . I am a superstitious person but this path of reasoning was beyond me. Here are just a few of the old wives tales I heard:

If you are carrying high (your boobs rest on your belly) then it's a girl; if you are carrying low (like a really exaggerated beer belly) then it's a boy. If you're carrying all around (gaining weight everywhere) then it's a girl; if you're carrying out in front (can't tell from behind) then it's a boy. If your legs get more hairy (Sasquatch), or your pee gets brighter yellow ('80s neon) then it's a boy. Sweet cravings and a high fetal heart rate mean girl.

There are some other non-physical indicators as well. There are charts and calendars that compare your age with the month of conception to predict the baby's sex. Some theories are just plain crazy. If you pick up a mug by its handle then you're having a boy; if you pick it up by the body of the mug then you're having a girl. I say that has less to do with the sex of my baby and more to do with whether or not my hands are cold. And some say babies are more likely to be born just after a full moon. I say only if you're giving birth to a werewolf although my grandfather, expert on all things (sincerely), swears this is true. Apparently just like the phases of the moon affect the tides, it has a similar effect on a pregnant woman's body due to all the extra fluid she's carrying. It's not the craziest I've heard so I'll buy into it.

Regardless of the means you use to find out, some people feel that they absolutely have to know. They say they need to plan and coordinate everything. I am a huge planner, and very organized, but that was one surprise I wanted to experience at the time of birth. Even if you do find out, you have to decide if you want to tell everyone else, or keep that little secret between you and your partner. And don't paint the nursery pink yet—those predictions are not always accurate.

Chapter 5

The Name Game

Finding out the sex of the baby does give you the advantage of narrowing the name search a little bit. If you're confident that you're having a girl then you can just focus on choosing the best possible name for her instead of going through the effort of compiling a list of boy names. Or maybe your list is too narrow to begin with.

There were very few names that my husband and I agreed on. As fast as one of us would sit up excitedly and yell out the name, the other would shoot it down. Having a "right to veto" rule with your partner has its pros and cons. Sure it pares the list down to mutual favorites but in doing so the name you've been saving since you were eight years old may have been eliminated. If too many names are rejected, your list dwindles quickly and you've heard "Veto" so often that you're left wondering if that's a good name.

You can get so caught up in the negative associations that you have to certain names. You don't want your son to carry the name of the neighborhood bully or the little brat you used to babysit. And clearly your daughter can't have the same name as the chick your husband used to live with (hopefully before he was your husband). Once other people start voicing their objections it's over. There will literally be no names left.

Family names, trendy names, traditional names . . . there has to be *something* you can agree on. And if you end up hating it, or decide it doesn't fit her personality, you can always come up with a cute nickname. Just don't overanalyze it. It's best to contemplate a name for a little while but not to pore over it for too long.

Appropriate Level of Analysis: You don't name your son Aiden Scott because your last name is Stevenson and A.S.S. is never a good monogram.

Exaggerated, Unnecessary Level of Analysis: You don't name your daughter Delilah because you don't want her associated with a biblical whore.

Don't get too out of control. Keep those crazy pregnancy hormones in check. You don't want your baby named after the brand of pretzels you were addicted to during your pregnancy. Let someone else censor the names that spontaneously pop into your head while you're up peeing at 3 am. Start with your all time favorites and pepper in a few new finds for consideration. Go with your gut—you'll learn to trust it for a lot of decisions.

~Chapter 6~

Nesting

Instinctually you'll start to feel like a mother before the baby is even born. You'll enjoy the tasks that are associated with preparing for the baby. Laundry is remarkably more fun when you're washing adorable onesies and teeny socks. Cleaning will take on a whole new meaning. Towards the end of your pregnancy you may feel the need not only to vacuum the carpet and scrub the bathroom like usual, but an irresistible urge to wash down the walls in your living room, and re-grout the bathroom tile . . . by hand, yourself.

Like many of the other odd tendencies of pregnancy, this is normal. It's called nesting — literally preparing a home for the baby. Some women find it sufficient to throw a fresh coat of paint on the walls in the spare bedroom, buy some baby furniture, and call it a day.

Others are not so laid back. Renovations are made. Walls are spackled, sanded, sealed, primed, and painted — but only after hundreds of color palates are scrutinized. Furniture is ordered, assembled, and placed with to-the-inch precision. Crib-sized bedding sets that cost more than my king size comforter are purchased. Strollers are researched extensively. The list — oh and there most certainly is a list — goes on and on.

Your level of interest (read: insanity) is no reflection on how you'll be as a mother. Someone who spends countless hours and dollars on the baby's room is no better a mother than the one who arranges the hand-me-downs in a matter of hours. Regardless of how you choose to nest, it's likely that sometime before your due date you'll find yourself alone in the baby's room rocking in the glider, daydreaming about what she'll be like. And it's then that you'll know you're ready.

If you're having a Baby Shower, or you anticipate that people will want to buy you presents, you may want to register. Some think this is presumptuous but my feeling is that it benefits everyone. They get a helpful list of suggestions, you get what you want! Certainly no one is obligated to shop from it. Here's another place that your partner can get involved and get excited. (And after all that spackling and furniture assembly, doesn't he deserve it?!)

He can aim that little product scanner and pretend he's in his very own video game. Just don't let him get trigger-happy. Despite what the online lists and magazine tear-out checklists say, you don't need all that stuff. Of course there are some important necessities, but the rest is just an overabundance of needless things and can more appropriately be called *excess*-ories.

It's so easy to get carried away but keep in mind that infancy is a transitional — and fleeting — time. You want plenty of the basics, like onesies and washcloths, since you don't want to do laundry all day long. However, now's not the time to follow the laws of abundance and get as much of everything as possible. Safety and practicality should be your guide. You'll regret buying that expensive swing when it evokes early signs of motion sickness rather than soothing the baby. Clothes won't be worn for more than a month or so, so don't save the cute outfit for a special occasion. You'll miss that small window of time when it fits and end up with a closet full of unworn clothes.

Of course you need a car seat to bring the baby home in. You need a safe place for the baby to sleep (there are endless possibilities — crib, bassinette, Moses' basket, cradle, etc.). You can worry about baby-proofing your house in a couple of months when he begins to move around on his own. Right now you have full control over where the baby is and what he's exposed to (this is a place to err on the side of caution). Your nesting instinct should have you well-prepared by time you go into labor.

Section Four

Labor and Delivery

Don't be so impatient!
Having the baby safely inside of you may prove easier
than having him out.

I gave birth at a teaching hospital so there was no shortage of extra hands or eyes in on the action (the "action" being what I had previously considered my private areas). When I arrived at the hospital I was taken in to be examined. They brought in a young male medical student who, under the strict supervision of his superior, would check my progress.

Having been through every doctor in a large practice and a rotating staff of nurses, I was accustomed to having relative strangers see me naked but this kid looked like he was twelve! He smirked as he checked for dilation, and sheepishly said, "Thank you" on his way out. I chalked it up to inexperience and embarrassment and giggled a little to myself. That was the last time I laughed for the following 22 hours.

~Chapter 1~

Pack Your Bags

You may have heard that you should pack a bag several weeks before your due date and keep it in the car. I think that's just crazy. What if you don't end up taking your car to the hospital? It's likely that you'll want to take your favorite and most comfortable clothes with you — and why would you want to live without them for the last couple weeks of your pregnancy? While it is a good idea to give some thought to what you'll want to take so that you're not scrambling around when the time comes, it's not the end of the world if you go to the hospital without an overnight bag.

The bag will just be one more thing for your partner to juggle as he helps your contracting body into the hospital. If it's your first pregnancy, you may go to the hospital several times before they actually admit you. (Just me? Oh, ok). Once you are there to stay, you'll be fitted with a gorgeous one of a kind gown. No, wait, that's wrong. It'll be one of a million ill-fitting snap-together drapes that countless other strangers have worn. In any case, that's what you'll wear throughout your time there so having your own clothes right away is not necessary.

Having a baby is messy. You and your partner will see and smell things in that room that you will likely not want to ever mention again. Unless you want your favorite sweatpants to tell the tale of your baby's delivery, don't bring them with you. And although I promised that you'll drop some weight quickly, don't bring your skinny jeans or anything else that will set you up for disappointment. Leave them at home, safely in your drawer.

Pack some underwear and bras (nursing bras if you plan to breastfeed), loose, comfortable shirts and pants, a bath towel and some toiletries. Remind your partner to bring pajamas, a toothbrush, and a change of clothes if he'll be staying with you (as if you'd allow him to leave you there alone).

We threw some snacks, a book, and an mp3 player in the bag as well. (Leave the crosswords and sudokus at home. You will not have the presence of mind to play!) A little entertainment can be a good distraction from labor pains and can help avoid the feeling that the hospital walls are closing in on you after a couple days.

Chapter 2

Party of 2 . . . soon to be 3

If you invite others into the Delivery Room with you, magazines may not be necessary. Having company may be distraction enough. It was my personal choice to keep our party private. I limited the number of people to my husband and me and the necessary medical personnel. Although I highly recommend having someone with you—either to coach you or just be there for moral support—I don't understand the desire to have your extended family and entire circle of friends with you in the delivery room. If they weren't there for the conception, they don't need to be there for the delivery. Only those who were in the room when you got pregnant should be in the room for the delivery.

Some things are sacred and I believe childbirth is one of them. The time my husband and I spent together in the delivery room was special; nothing topped seeing his face as he said, "It's a boy! We have a boy!" The doctors, nurses, and techs seemed to disappear at that moment but I can't imagine the same could be said if family and friends had been present.

Although it wasn't my choice, I can understand wanting to share the experience with your sister, best friend, mom, or someone similar. Whatever you decide, make sure they are aware of your plans, as well as the fact that they could change at any moment. You want to be surrounded by those who can calm you in moments of fear, not cause you panic. And remember—you have the right to eject anyone for any reason at any time.

~Chapter 3~

The Eleventh Hour

The room is ready, the car seat is secured rear-facing in the backseat, the closet is full, you've taken the classes; there's just one more thing to do. One simple little thing. Well, hopefully simple. It's time to have that baby.

As your due date grows near you may realize that actually *having* a baby is the one thing you forgot to think about. Or maybe you've had your birth plan coordinated and documented for months. Either way, unless you have a scheduled due date, you have little control over when the baby is actually born.

Of all the things you've supplied your baby with over the last nine months, there's no calendar in there. A due date is an estimation of the completion of your pregnancy, but many women take their due date as bible. I always regarded my due date as a deadline, but it's rare that your baby's due date and birthday happen to be on the same day. Although it can be hard not to become anxious and impatient, it's best not to rush. Babies are born when they're ready. Mine were each ready six days after their due dates.

Unless your doctor finds a reason to speed things along, he may let things take their natural course. That could mean you staying pregnant for up to two more weeks. Just when you thought you had reached the end, that reward gets pushed back a little farther. There's one thing you can be sure of though — one way or another, that baby's coming out. And at this point, it's only a matter of time.

There are many ways to bring on labor. Just like conception methods and gender predictions, those old wives have something to say about coaxing your body into labor. Eating spicy foods may help launch you into labor . . . or so they say. There is no scientific research to back this one. Also, vomiting can sometimes accompany progress so don't eat anything that you'd mind seeing a repeat performance of. A triple bean burrito may not be something you want to see again.

Castor oil, an old fashioned cure-all remedy, is credited with nudging labor along. If you can manage to swallow this unpleasant-tasting liquid, make sure you stay within waddling range of a bathroom. Traditionally used as a laxative, castor oil causes spasms of the intestines that may cause uterine contractions. However strong, they may not be "real" contractions but instead can put undue stress on the baby.

Perhaps the safest, and potentially most effective methods, are sex and walking. A chemical found in sperm can help your cervix efface and stimulate contractions. It may be the last time you and your partner can make love for the next several weeks so even if it doesn't help, it's not all for nothing.

Taking a stroll around the block may help your body prepare for delivery. Pregnancy hormones have been softening your muscles and joints over the past several months. Walking naturally exercises your hips and pelvis, helping them to loosen and relax. Plus, light exercise can actually give you more energy — energy that you'll need for the days to come.

No matter how anxious you are to meet your baby (and reclaim your body as your own, sort of), safety should be your utmost concern when considering any labor-inducing activities. While most tricks are harmless, taking medications — even herbal — can be very dangerous. Consult with your physician before taking *anything*.

Sometimes babies are smarter than you know. Not arriving promptly on their due date could be an indication that they're not physically ready yet. So relax and let your little Einstein develop into the picture of perfection that you've been anticipating.

If there is a medical reason to get the baby out, he'll likely discuss scheduling a date for a Caesarean Section or Induction. Your doctor will be able to recommend the best course of action once he assesses your situation. For now, just take comfort in the fact that you've provided such a nice warm, comfy home for the past nine months, that your baby isn't ready to come out! You can't blame 'em. Do you like to toss your comforter aside and climb out of bed on a cold winter morning?

~Chapter 4~

It's Go Time

When the time finally comes, whether your water broke, your contractions match the pattern they told you about, or it's the morning of your scheduled delivery, you might suddenly decide you're not ready. Here's when you need to take a deep breath and accept that it's happening. At this point childbirth is unavoidable; there's no postponing it any longer.

It's completely understandable that you're not ready. Whether you're scared of delivering the baby, or being a parent to a child living outside of your body, it's a daunting task to face. Labor and Delivery, often called L&D, is nothing like the other commonly-used abbreviation R&R (rest and relaxation)!

The details of your hospital stay are largely determined by the practices of that facility. The hospital where I delivered my sons had a Labor and Delivery Triage Unit where they checked to make sure I was actually in real labor, and then monitored my progress until the baby and I seemed almost ready. At that point, we moved to the L&D Room where I labored and ultimately delivered.

The room was beautiful, like a luxury suite at a hotel. Even through my contraction-induced haze I noticed the high ceiling, the private full bathroom, the soothing wall color, the beautiful modern paintings on the wall, and most of all the floors. My husband was seriously thinking about asking what brand of hardwood flooring it was so that we could install it in our dining room.

Then the conversion began. I didn't know if I should be amazed or scared. The artwork swung on a hinge like a door, revealing oxygen masks and other stuff I couldn't identify. A remote lowered a huge light from the vaulted ceiling. It was impressive. Now where was the magic wand that took the pain away?

I was determined to hold out as long as I could but the contractions would rise and begin to fall, and then start to rise again when they got only halfway back down. I couldn't get a break. I couldn't catch my breath. The nurse told me I was doing a great job breathing through the contractions but her praise was little consolation. My husband didn't know what to do; he knew the decision was mine.

Then, with the shift change of the nurses, I had a change of my own. When I started throwing up about three-quarters of the way into the 22 hour labor that eventually produced our first son, my husband called the nurses into the room. I had gotten up to pee and started simultaneously puking orange Jell-o (the only thing I had eaten in 18 hours), leaking amniotic fluid (they had broken my water to try to coax him out), and shaking uncontrollably.

55

The nurse came in, glanced at me, and turned back around and left. Between my sobs I heard her tell the other nurse, "She's just tossing her cookies." She could have reminded me that these were things that could happen during transition — something I had forgotten in my current state. Instead, she downplayed our concern. Everyone knows that condescension is not well received in general, but even less so by a woman in labor. If the attitude of your L&D nurse makes her seem more suited for S&M, ignore her. She's just desensitized.

Moments later I "gave in" and rang for the nicer nurse. I was ready for the epidural. So they called in the anesthesiologist (apparently he's the one with the magic wand). For some reason I was a little disappointed in myself. I was treating it as a battle of wills, testing my pain threshold. If I knew it would have been over in one more hour I could have held out, but after 18 hours it still seemed like the end was nowhere in sight.

There's no shame in having an epidural — or any other form of pain intervention. There's no trophy for going natural, so don't do it for the badge of honor. Follow your body's natural cues. Although certain drugs can slow your progress, it won't go quickly if you're too tired to push either. You don't have to follow a pre-determined plan that was made before you knew how you'd react. It's ok to change your mind.

Forget what you've heard. The epidural is not bad. It definitely hurts less than contractions. The hardest part is sitting still during contractions. Once it's in, the level of drugs can be adjusted. Most likely it'll be turned down when it's time to push. Mine was. I didn't feel pain, but I could feel pressure — which helped me know when, and how hard, to push.

Oh yes, pushing — the beginning of the end, the lead up to the grand finale of childbirth. I was instructed to bear down through my bottom. Let me translate: Push like you're pooping. Speaking of pooping, if you haven't heard yet, that can happen while you're pushing. Trust me, it's not the grossest thing that will come out of you. And you won't be the first one to do it. You probably won't even be the first one that day. This was ever-present on my mind throughout the whole process. Just what I needed, something else to worry about. I didn't think that it happened but it wasn't until weeks later that I confirmed that with my husband. After all, he had a much better vantage point than I did.

No one has a better vantage point than your doctor. Although there will likely be many other medical personnel in the room (who are all these people?!), she's the one who has the front row ticket. They say they don't notice unshaved legs or bikini areas (who can reach after the sixth month?) but I have proof that their attention is not always focused front and center.

My doctor noticed, and commented on, my manicured nails as my hands were hooked behind my legs, holding them up so I could push. I told her that it was done when my best friend had treated me once my due date came and went, but what I wanted to tell her was to focus on the task at hand so we could get it over with!

Luckily, I didn't have to push for very long. I guess I have a strong vagina (I'm adding it to my resume). Also, I followed the nurse's instructions, "Take a deep breath, hold it, and push as hard as you can." It hurts, it's hard, scream if you want—but not while you're pushing. That's wasted energy. Shut your mouth and push. Harsh, I know, but you'll thank me later.

Oh, and congratulations. You just gave birth to a beautiful new baby.

~Chapter 5~

The Morning After

As a new parent, it is your responsibility and obligation to let everyone know. This usually involves calling your closest family members and friends to give sex, height, and weight details, along with a brief description of the birth. From there, the word is spread to others via whichever top level person is the most excited /can dial the fastest/ knows the most people.

Other, more obsessive, people make a spreadsheet and pack it in their hospital bag. It is so important that it dare not be handwritten, but rather printed out and possibly even laminated. It includes family and friends, home and cell numbers, each carefully arranged in the order in which people should be called—and during what hours it is ok to call.

I admittedly fell into the second category. *I should call my aunt before my friend because she's family*, I thought as my husband got my phone from my purse. What it really comes down to is that no one will document the time you called so the other will be none the wiser. Recipients of such great news should be happy for you, not concerned with which tier of importance they fell into. Call whomever you want. Or, take a few minutes to stare at your new baby. You went in to that room as a couple, but you're leaving as a family. You may need a minute for that to sink in.

The morning after I got engaged, my ring caught my eye as I woke up and I thought, "Oh my God, I'm getting married!" I had a similar reaction the first time I woke up after my son was born. It wasn't the next morning; it was approximately 90 minutes after I had finally closed my eyes for the first time in about 40 hours. When a tech came in to take my vitals, I woke up and wondered for a split second where I was. And then I felt that pinching pain when I tried to sit up and remembered, "Oh right, I had a baby." Not that I forgot—it was kind of like the first night of vacation when you wake up to pee and it takes a few moments to realize that you're in a hotel instead of your own room.

There will be little time over the next couple days (18+ years?) to let anything sink in. The next few hours or days may be a blur. Emotions, pain, lack of sleep, and sheer joy can easily cloud your mind. Add a new tiny baby, visitors, and a parade of nurses armed with blood pressure cuffs and 800mg ibuprophen, and you may just be too overwhelmed to remember what you named the baby (and you know what a process that was).

Among the things that may hit you are: how your partner is much better at calming the baby than you anticipated (admit it, you were nervous), how disgusting it is to not be allowed to wipe yourself (but the squirt bottle of water feels better than hospital-grade toilet paper), how — once you identified him — you realized that your baby is so much cuter than all the other kids in the nursery (how sad for the other parents), how your legs are much skinnier than you remember (maybe just in comparison to the cankles you developed around month seven).

These seem like a lot of random shallow thoughts, but when combined with trying to remember which side you last fed the baby on, and how on earth you're going to handle all this, it can be quite scary. If you're overwhelmed, just rely on your partner, the nurses, or your family for help. It may take some adjusting, but the past nine months have prepared you for this.

~Chapter 6~

Have a Look, Everyone Else Has — Your Postpartum Checkup

Embarrassment is one thing that won't faze you. Having abandoned your modest nature somewhere amid the doctor's appointments, and having left all shreds of dignity in the delivery room, you won't even blink when your doctor or nurse comes in to check your episiotomy stitches or your hemorrhoids. You'll continue to eat your cup of rice pudding (the only edible thing on your hospital tray), and think about how damn good your legs are gonna' look this summer.

Don't be so distracted that you forget to ask questions though. Your delivery may have been a blur — all 16 hours of it. Medication aside, the rush of emotions and endorphins may have left you asking to hear, instead of telling, stories from the delivery room. If you have questions about anything that happened, good or bad, now is the time to speak up. Your doctor can likely answer all of your questions and provide a reason for last minute changes. If you haven't had quite enough time to recover and your mind is still cloudy, you may need more time to process everything that happened. Call your doctor once you're home, or make a few notes that you can take to your postpartum check up.

Depending on your birthing method, you'll likely return to the doctor's office that you once visited so often, for one final maternity exam. He'll check your weight (don't be scared) and blood pressure. The abdominal exam will ensure that your belly is not unusually tender, and that your uterus has returned to its previous size (about as big as a pear). He'll check your breasts for lumps, abnormal discharge, or infections, whether you're breastfeeding or not.

For the first time since perhaps the beginning of your pregnancy, he'll do a speculum exam, and possibly do a Pap smear. He can make sure any tears or incisions are healing properly, including episiotomies. During an internal exam he'll feel your uterus and ovaries, and may do a rectal exam also (does the fun ever end?).

Provided that everything checks out alright, you'll probably be given the go ahead to start having sex again. This may be the one restriction that you'd welcome for another few weeks (or years). Many moms aren't exactly ready to jump in the sack the moment the sex ban is lifted. Even so, unless you're ready for round two already, talk to him about birth control options.

Your doctor will likely ask how you're adjusting to life as a new mom. With post-pregnancy hormones beginning to regulate, your fluctuating emotions may start to normalize. You want to make sure that they stay at the happy end of the spectrum.

Section Five

Life After Birth

Your life will never again be the same — and that's a good thing

Where did this kid come from and when does he leave? Even after nine months of pregnancy and several hours of labor, you may feel as though someone unexpectedly dropped a baby in your arms. Since this little package didn't come with a gift receipt, he's yours to keep so you need to adjust.

Some mothers instantly feel a bond with their baby, for others that relationship takes some cultivation. Try not to let preconceived notions of how you *should* feel affect how you *actually* feel. It's normal to feel inadequate — you have been suddenly thrown into the hardest job in the world with very little instruction — and alienated — despite all the people who want to visit, very few understand what you're feeling.

~Chapter 1~

Baby Blues and Frozen Lasagnas

Once you make it home from the hospital (an exceptionally slow ride due to the new precious cargo) you may find yourself surprisingly uncomfortable. I'm not referring to your burning stitches, but rather the feeling that you have no idea what to do with your new addition. At some point you'll have to get her out of the baby carrier and introduce her to her new home.

Starving after rejecting three days of hospital food, you likely be too nervous to eat. Even if you are looking forward to dinner, good luck eating while crying. I don't know why you'll be crying. You won't even know why you're crying. It just happens. Maybe the baby woke up just as you managed to lower yourself into a chair. Maybe you're overcome with joy. Happy tears or sad tears, keep the tissues on hand.

It's unrealistic to say you'll get a good night's sleep, but once you make it through the first night and realize everyone survived, you may start to feel some sense of confidence beginning to resurface. Maybe you'll even be up for company. Don't overdo it. Now is not the time to vie for Hostess of the Year. Make it clear that you will not be changing out of your pajamas or waking the baby for the sake of a visitor.

Most people will understand and will not be offended in the least. In fact, many well-wishers may come bearing food, and ready to help. Your freezer may soon be stocked with casseroles and lasagnas . . . lots of lasagnas. Accept each duplicative Pyrex dish graciously and let them do whatever household chore they offer. While it may not be the appropriate time to get picky (telling them you like your towels folded lengthwise and *then* widthwise), it is ok to accept help.

Some women have their mother or sister move in for a couple weeks, others have sporadic visitors. I was never good at handing out jobs or sleeping while someone was at my house, but that's just my personal hang up. Anytime you have an opportunity to sleep while the baby is in safe hands, take it! While your support system may be strong, all the day to day help won't last very long.

Within two weeks of bringing the baby home, the phone calls and visits will likely decrease. You may have had your partner home with you for a week or so, depending on his employment situation but by time he has to go back to work, you'll likely start to be home alone more and more often. Although you are still ecstatic to be a new mom, the reality starts to set in. As the attention begins to fade away from you, and everyone else returns to business as normal, you're left alone to embark on this new journey into the great unknown.

This is an important time to pay attention to your feelings. It's normal to feel weepy and emotional but if you begin to have even the slightest inclination to harm yourself or the baby, get help immediately. Having these feelings or being overwhelmed to the point of hysteria does not make you a bad mother. You should not feel ashamed; seeking help in the form of therapy or medication is the responsible thing to do.

Just like the anxiety of trying to conceive, the challenges of pregnancy, and the pain of labor, this too will pass. You will soon fall into the swing of your new routine, establish a bond with your new baby that challenges all other relationships you've known, and forget what life was like without her. You may even feel more in love with her than anyone else in the world . . . to the detriment of only your partner.

~Chapter 2~

The Six Week Rule

It's recommended that you don't have sex for six weeks, or at least until you go back for your postpartum checkup and get the all clear. Supposedly that's so that you have time to heal and recover from the recent trauma to the key areas, but I think it's about more than that. First of all, unless you're the parent of the one in a million babies who are born knowing how to sleep and eat on schedule, you will not have time. It's more likely that you'll need to be reintroduced to your partner by time you're ready to have sex.

Amazingly, even after witnessing the beautiful mess called childbirth, your partner still finds you sexy. It would seem natural that after the memory of the Delivery Room scene, along with a whiff of your New Mom Smell, your partner won't want to be in sniffing range, much less close enough for any type of intimacy. New Mom Smell? That's the lovely scent combination of breast milk and unwashed hair. It's similar in concept to New Car Smell, only it's not as desirable and it doesn't fade as fast. But by some miracle of nature, he's not disgusted by you but rather has a really difficult time lasting through those seemingly-endless six weeks. We think we're a superior species, but we really are animals.

That's just his feelings about it. What about you? Maybe you enjoyed your legitimate excuse, sing-songing, "Sorry, we can't—Doctor's Orders" each time he came within three feet of you. It's most likely that you were just indifferent about it. While you're looking forward to, one day, having sex again, you don't want that day to be today . . . or tomorrow. During these days when it's hard to find time to brush your teeth, you may not even have had time to think about it at all.

Add in the potential for pain and you might be left wanting to extend your stay at Hotel Celibacy for another few weeks. It's one of life's nasty jokes that during your breasts' peak they're most untouchable. Between the potential pain and the risk of leakage, you'll be tempted to have 'Hands Off' printed on the cups—God knows there's plenty of room on that full coverage nursing bra.

A weakened pelvic floor (I told you to do those kegels!), stitches, and residual increased sensitivity can make that first time feel, well, like your first time. Unless it's unbearable, try, try again. Just like when you were pregnant, warn your partner to go slow and take it easy and experiment with different positions. Don't let your body be a buzzkill. While you may be horrified at the idea of getting into any position that risks letting your new excess belly skin hang down, you can be sure that's not what your partner is focusing on.

~Chapter 3~

She Has a Nice Body . . . for a Mom

I would give anything to have my high school body back. I have often heard women say this. Not me. Sure my boobs were a little perkier (ok, a lot perkier), but just like I don't want the hairstyle, fashion choices, or high school drama back, I don't want the body either. To start, I didn't really love my body in high school; those were not my best body days. Others would agree.

About two months after my first son was born, I went to a school reunion. A guy I had gone to both grade school and high school with gave me one of the most back-handed compliments I have ever received. "You look so different," he said, looking me up and down. "You look *good.*" So during the twelve years that we spent together in school I looked what? something other than good?

At first, my body could be attributed to my not-exactly-rigorous regimen of breastfeeding and stroller walks around the block. My stomach had gotten so big during my second pregnancy that I had an abdominal diastasis (separation of stomach muscles) and wasn't allowed to lift anything heavy or do most ab exercises. And that was a good excuse for me not to do anything. Although I was concerned that my body would never be the same, I was not compelled to do much about it.

My post-baby workout consisted of running (to the phone to avoid missing a chance to talk to an adult), jumping (up in the middle of the night to make sure the baby was still breathing), skipping (a shower when I ran out of time), lifting (8lbs 6oz about 198 times a day), stretching (for the remote without detaching the baby from my breast), and crunches (pretzels, not abs).

Much to my shock and pleasure, I dropped my baby weight unexpectedly quickly and amazingly easily. The swelling that had given my ankles the same circumference as my knees went away almost immediately. The water weight was gone by the time I left the hospital and many of the actual pounds followed quickly thereafter. I actually looked forward to being weighed at my six week postpartum check up. (My estimate was right. I was 4 pounds heavier than my starting weight—and clearly that could be accounted for by boob weight!)

I was back in my regular clothes within weeks. They didn't fit the same way that they had in the past, but I could button them and still look acceptable (not-too-shabby if I do say so myself). My new mom body didn't look the same as my pre-pregnancy body (clothes hide a lot), but I was ok with that. The number on the scale was not my main concern, although I knew that my weight consisted of many more fat pounds and many less muscle pounds than the previous ratio.

My stomach, once my favorite, most prized body part, had been replaced with a belly. But again, these things were more than acceptable just two months after having a baby.

Fitting In Working Out

Four, six, eight months later, I was not as pleased. My body was in the same shape that it was in at two months postpartum, maybe worse. Posture, strength, endurance . . . they were all things of the past. Something needed to be done, and that something required a little sweat. I knew that it would take some exercise to reclaim a semi-flat stomach, even if it would never again have bounce-a-quarter-off-it status. My frame of mind changed quickly from smug to desperate. Too bad my desire to work out was not revived as quickly as my vanity.

After not working out for so long I knew I needed to start slow, although maybe not as slow as I did. Three minutes into my first real workout (pushing the stroller around the block no longer qualified as a workout), I had to stop. The support that my old sports bra provided was nowhere near sufficient. I knew that jumping around without support would not help my already saggy situation. Shopping was a much easier activity to get back into than exercise.

Two new and improved, larger than life, sports bras later, I was ready to try again. I changed into my workout clothes and even got my feet, which had grown all too used to slippers and flip flops, back into my sneakers. Once the baby fell asleep I'd be off and running—more like jumping and squatting actually. Soon I realized that what I had been hearing all these years really is true—somehow working out actually *gives* you energy. That is against all logic but is true.

There's no way I could have done it two months earlier. My body wasn't healed and I was so tired from being up several times a night. But now I was ready. I was doing it and, as much as I hate to admit it, I was liking it. Soon, I was not only liking the workout, but enjoying the results. My muscle memory was a big help, although it was more of a walk down memory lane rather than total recall. My stomach muscles began to tighten and started to resemble their previous form. I gained endurance, and confidence. And confidence looks good on anyone. I decided to stick with that mom body. And with a little bit of work, I learned to love it after all.

I was conscious of what I ate during my pregnancy, but I know that I was very, *very* lucky. It takes nine months to put on the weight, so it may take that long (or more) to shed those pounds. If you treat pregnancy as a feeding frenzy, don't expect the pounds to fly off like a popped balloon. No matter what condition your body ends up in, it's unlikely that you'll regret having a baby. I know I don't.

~Chapter 4~

Nursing 101:
Breastfeeding Basics

The American Academy of Pediatrics recommends that babies be breast-fed for six to twelve months (the only appropriate alternative being formula). Not everyone can, or chooses to, nurse at all. Others do it for as long as they want, maybe only a couple months.

I would say it is, at least, worth considering. In fact, I think breastfeeding is the best thing ever (chocolate is made with milk, milk comes from boobs, so we're covered here). Sure it can be hard (seemingly impossible) at first, and tiring (plain old exhausting) at times, but there are so many advantages. The nutritional and emotional benefits that it affords both you and your child are outstandingly remarkable, it's cheaper, you're self-sufficient, your stomach goes down, and you get stripper boobs (that's right).

Doing It "Right"

A lactation consultant, basically a certified breastfeeding expert, may be your best friend for the duration of your hospital stay. She can help you with what is your most important job right now — nourishing your baby. She can explain about the properties of colostrum when you're worried that what seems like dribbles of honey aren't enough to satisfy your baby. By helping you position the baby for the most ideal latch, she can actually help your milk come in.

Colostrum is the first form of milk that is produced by your mammary glands. It is very concentrated so even a very small amount can provide many nutrients for your baby. You should try to introduce your baby to the breast as soon after delivery as possible, and frequently thereafter. This will help increase the production of your mature milk, often referred to as making your milk come in. The baby's sucking will stimulate that milk to increase in volume and consistency. Within a few days you'll notice that your milk is more plentiful (note the firm, round boobies) and more closely resembles milk as you know it — thinner than the colostrum, and almost opaque white.

The baby may be sleepy at first, or seem uninterested in feeding. Persistence and patience are of the essence right now! Brush the baby's lips with your nipple, or express a little milk to dribble into her mouth (ask your lactation consultant for help if you need it). These tricks may help your baby open her mouth and become more receptive. A proper latch — the way your baby takes your nipple into her mouth — is essential for the baby's nutrition and your comfort. An incorrect latch can quickly lead to sore nipples.

Hold her so that she is facing you with her shoulders and hips in a line. It is important that both you and she are comfortable. Although it looks off-center, align your baby's nose with your nipple, her chin angled slightly upward. Once your baby's mouth is open, gently but firmly pull her towards your breast. It sounds strange, but that's what makes everything end up in the right place!

Soon, she won't need help at all, she'll be chomping at the bit . . . so to speak. You'll notice that her lips are rolled out, not tucked under or sucked in, and you'll see or hear her swallowing. You should feel a tugging sensation but it should not be painful. If you need to readjust her latch don't just pull her away. A baby's suction is very strong so she'll likely stay attached and end up pulling your nipple with her. Instead, use your finger to gently poke the corner of her mouth to break the seal. She'll open her mouth and you can give her another chance to latch correctly. Repeat this as necessary.

The way you hold your baby can affect her latch. There are some positions that can angle her head and help her achieve a correct latch. The cradle hold is perhaps the most commonly used position. As the name suggests, you cradle the baby in your arms with her head alongside your bicep or resting in the bend of your elbow, depending on her size. She'll feel cozy and connected, and this will encourage a good feeding session.

The football hold is somewhat of a reversal of the cradle hold. Support the baby's head in the palm of your hand with her body lying on your inner arm. Her legs will be slightly wrapped around your side. If you've never held a football, it may be difficult to imagine; the baby will be entirely on the same side of your body as the breast on which she's nursing. This position can be good for mothers who had a C-section as it keeps the weight of the baby off of your abdomen. It can also be good for women with large breasts.

It's also possible to nurse the baby while lying down. With both of you lying on your sides, belly to belly, she'll nurse on your lower breast. You may need to support your breast or the baby's head with your opposite hand. This is convenient if your baby sleeps in bed with you, or for those times that you've already been up ten times and no longer trust yourself to safely hold the baby in your arms!

How often your baby wants to nurse is not always strictly dependant on how hungry she is. Some prefer to nurse on-demand for at least the first few weeks. Doing this will give you an idea of the baby's feeding pattern, and will help regulate your milk supply. Babies have very strong hungry and full senses so if she seems uninterested there's no need to force a feeding (of course if your baby is underweight, consistently refuses the breast, or has other health issues, talk to your doctor). The snuggle time with mommy and the act of sucking are very pleasing to a baby so sometimes they want to nurse for comfort or to help them get to sleep. As with everything, there are differing opinions on this. Do whatever works best for you and your baby.

You may be surprised to see that milk comes out of several holes, like a watering can. It was certainly an unexpected realization for me. However, the biggest surprise may be how you don't feel put out by breastfeeding. You may actually enjoy it and feel fulfilled (physically and emotionally!). After hearing about engorgement and cracked nipples, you might be shocked when it doesn't hurt. You might not be as self-conscious about nursing the baby in the company of others, and you may even be sad to wean. A note about weaning: the right time to wean your baby is a personal decision that can be affected by physical, emotional, or cultural factors, among other reasons. Be sure that you stop for the right reasons—not because you feel embarrassed. That being said, there will definitely come a time (well before starting Kindergarten!) that your child is old enough and healthy enough to drink from a bottle or cup.

HEALTH BENEFITS (FOR YOU AND BABY)

The Perfect Food

Breast milk or formula will be the mainstay of nutrition for the baby's full first year. Even after you introduce him to the array of gourmet purees that baby food has become, a large part of his sustenance should be from breast milk or formula (not cow's milk) at least until his first birthday.

Not only is breast milk the ideal food—containing perfect amounts of water, lactose, and fatty acids, and the amino acids necessary for brain development and proper growth (not to mention over 100 ingredients that are not found in even the most advanced formula)—it is also a miracle drug.

A breastfed baby is a healthy baby! The US FDA reports lower rates of ear infections, diarrhea, rashes, allergies, and other medical issues than bottle-fed babies. Aside from staving off a whole host of illnesses, a mother's milk contains antibodies that will help protect her baby from any germs to which she has been exposed. For that reason, breastfeeding even while you're sick is approved, and even encouraged. So while you are not thrilled to be nursing the worst summer cold you've ever had and a baby at the same time, you can rest assured that you're getting Mommy of the Year points. (I know—*rest assured*? When was the last time you rested at all, much less did it in a confident way?!)

Other than the physical health benefits, nursing may be beneficial to the baby's emotional and psychological development as well. Breastfeeding promotes and nurtures a strong bond between you and your baby. (Sometimes too strong; have you ever tried to break the seal of a baby's mouth around a nipple?!) Sucking encourages both physical and emotional development. Although a baby can only see about 10-15 inches away for the first several days of life, his mother's face is still within sight while breastfeeding. With his vision limited, a baby relies on his other senses, just as a blind man would.

Sound and smell are particularly utilized. Babies soon learn to turn their head at the sound of their mother's voice. Studies have found that infants as young as one week prefer the smell of their own mother's milk. Whether they can recognize their own mother's milk or not, breastfed babies definitely know the smell of milk. More than once, I have held friends' babies and had him or her dive for my breast. They're like little bloodhounds. They know what it is and they know where to find it.

Mother's Health Benefits

Not only is breastfeeding great for your baby's health and development, it can have amazing effects on your long-term health and well-being as well. The cancer rates—particularly "women's cancers" such as ovarian, uterine, and breast—are found to be lower in women who have breastfed. In a world where everyone knows someone who has been afflicted with cancer, nursing your baby seems like one of the easiest preventive measures.

Oxytocin is a hormone that is secreted during labor and while breastfeeding. It gives mothers that warm and fuzzy feeling, helping them and the baby get through labor. One study suggests that, during delivery, oxytocin has an affect on a baby's brain cells, reducing their need for oxygen, and even helps calm their pain receptors. After delivery, it helps with the bonding process, as it is continually released while the baby eats at the breast.

FRINGE BENEFITS

The Perks

Putting the ever-important factors of the health benefits and increased bonding time that breastfeeding offers aside, the great rack is perhaps my favorite (and most selfish) reward. They're so round and firm—I call them stripper boobs due to their huge size, high positioning, and hard quality—but are still natural-looking.

But nursing is not just good for your boobs, it does wonderful things for your body too. With a couple hundred calories a day going to the baby, it's like dieting without the willpower normally required. Breastfeeding causes your uterus to contract and shrink, therefore helping your belly to go down. With workouts prohibited by physical restrictions and lack of spare time (or interest), this is a great thing. I have seen it time and again and really believe it is one of nature's little gifts to moms.

A Free Meal / No Brownbag Required

The recent advances in baby formula are amazing. There should be no guilt in giving your baby formula. That being said, that stuff is *expensive*! Breastfeeding is free. Plus, your baby's lunch is completely self-contained; no bottles, powder, or water to take along. I don't nurse in public (personal modesty preference, not because I care if it disgusts anyone else) so the most I had to do was find a bathroom, dressing room, or other semi-private area.

THE DOWNSIDE OF NURSING

Safe Sex . . . sort of

You can't get pregnant when you're nursing. Seems like a perk, right? Sure, except that it's not entirely true. Nursing is a natural contraceptive—although not a very reliable one. Ovulation is suppressed by consistent and frequent nursing. Without ovulation there are no eggs to be fertilized, therefore making it seemingly impossible to get pregnant. *Seemingly* impossible—but not *actually* impossible.

Just because you're not getting your period doesn't mean that there's not work going on behind the scenes. The uterine lining is completely shed after birth and it may take a few months to rebuild. Menstruation is sometimes delayed for the entire time you breastfeed. This can give you a false sense of safety, but the same over-confidence that causes you to toss the condoms aside may be deflated when you find yourself accidentally pregnant just in time for your newborn's four month birthday.

If you don't want to be pregnant again, don't take the chance. Talk to your doctor about contraception that is safe to use while breastfeeding. Although I'm sure he wants your repeat business, a hysterical woman screaming, "But I was breastfeeding!" may not be his ideal patient.

Nipple Confusion

Nipple confusion is a term that is often used to refer to the trouble a baby can have switching back and forth between the breast and a bottle. Like so many of these terms, I think there's a different, much more applicable meaning. Perhaps it used to be that your breasts were most admired by your partner. Now that they are the sole source of food for your child, your partner's desire pales in comparison to that of your baby. They are at the beck and call of hunger cries, rewarded only with maybe a little lanolin cream here and there. Between their newfound purpose and new #1 fan, you'll be left wondering who those little pencil-eraser-looking-things belong to anyway.

I always maintained a strong separation of the functional and sexual aspects of breasts. Breastfeeding just never had a sexual association for me. Some women are creeped out by the idea of their child sucking at their nipple. It is sometimes considered weirder to nurse a son because of the thought that some day he will be a big strong man with a partner of his own. Others think it's more unusual to nurse a daughter since they are the same sex. Try to keep in mind that although the same organs that make you a woman also make you a mother, there is nothing perverse about breastfeeding. It is completely natural. The throbbing feeling of engorgement, toe curling pain of an incorrect latch, and nipples cracking in rebellion can be quite obvious reminders that it is not a sexual act!

Veins Like a Roadmap, Nipples Pointing East and West

A good friend of mine came over to see my newborn and immediately said, "Oh my goodness, look at your boobs! They're beautiful!" I was pretty proud. Not since the popular cheerleader from high school have I seen a sweater filled out so nicely.

The ugly little secret is that under that sweater is a roadmap of blue veins that I personally think is a little unnecessary (after all, babies are born knowing where to get their next meal). And my nipples, most often sticking out through even the thickest bra, are slightly angled out toward my biceps thanks to the way my son liked to turn his head, but I'd say any pain or inconvenience you encounter during start up (the first couple weeks) is far outweighed by all the perks (no pun intended. Well, maybe a little pun).

You're On Your Own

With a couple weeks of practice you can usually nurse the baby without anyone in the room even knowing. But if you're modest, or in the company of gawkers, you may be forced to either go in the other room or show everyone your goods. Even the most dedicated mother can feel bitter about being exiled to a secluded back room during a party.

You may like the fact that you control your baby's eating schedule, and it eliminates the fight over who gets to give the baby his bottle. But that also means that you're on your own. No one else can help you feed the baby—at least not without pumping.

My Love Affair with the Pump

If nursing is the epitome of natural, then pumping is the epitome of unnatural. I immediately found it to be awkward and uncomfortable. The packaging said it was whisper quiet (it wasn't) and could mimic the rhythm of the baby (it couldn't). But I was committed to, and a little obsessed with, making it work.

It turned out that the manual attachment to my expensive automatic electric pump worked best for me. Unfortunately, once opened, breast pumps are not returnable so you can't keep trying until you find one you like. They are available for rent from hospitals and groups such as La Leche League. Or, if a friend had success with one and isn't using it anymore, you can buy your own hosing or attachments and borrow hers. That way, if it doesn't work for you, you have spent a much smaller amount of money.

When I was nursing my second son, my let down was much stronger and my love affair with the pump was a much more, uh, fluid relationship. Even though it was physically easier, finding time to pump was much more difficult with an older child at home as well. Here's hoping that the image of his mother pumping fades as he gets older.

Discretion was not my main priority at home. However, I did try to be somewhat inconspicuous once I went back to work. I kept my pump and its supplies in a padded thermal lunch bag. The filled bottles fit in there as well; I didn't feel comfortable sliding my breast milk-filled bottle onto the shelf next to my co-workers lunches (egg salad sandwiches and cupcakes are not good company for my liquid gold anyway). Several of the women knew but that was mainly because I took more than my share of turns in the Ladies' Room several times a day.

If you didn't particularly like being sequestered in another room to nurse your baby, then you'll likely hate hanging out in the bathroom with a machine designed to milk you like a cow. Excuse me if I'm being melodramatic — it seemed worse some days than others.

Pumping enough to fill a bottle for the babysitter to feed the baby while you go out to an occasional dinner is one thing, trying to maintain a breast milk-only feeding schedule while you work full time is quite another. If pumping does not produce enough milk to be worth it, or if you are simply not interested, supplementing the baby with formula while you're not together is an option. As long as you are routinely and regularly nursing, your milk supply should stay plentiful.

Disclaimer — A Woman's Right to Boobs

As an advocate of breastfeeding, I also understand that health issues, beliefs, or personal preferences may prevent you from it. Depending on your body, your newborn's interest, and your level of commitment, breastfeeding may not be easy for you. Your threshold for pain or willingness to stick with it may play a role also. It definitely takes persistence.

If the laundry list of benefits I gave you didn't convince you to give nursing a try then perhaps it's not for you. I'm done selling it — who am I to tell you what to do with your breasts?

Section Six

___

Settling In — A Couple
Months into Mommyhood

Record your baby's giggles, coos, or babbles. Those few moments captured in time will melt your heart in remembrance once he's speaking in sentences!

Some days seem so long, and nights even longer, but one day a calendar will catch your eye and you'll realize that months have gone by since you gave birth. By then you may have completely adjusted to life as a mom, probably won't remember what all the fuss was about, and may even be ready to start this baby process all over again! Or maybe not quite yet.

You will at least have realized that you have to roll with the punches. Being a mom means being flexible — literally and figuratively. You never get a day off. Even if the baby isn't in your immediate care every moment, you're still responsible overall. You can't even manage to enjoy a lazy weekend; babies don't know to sleep in on Sundays, and they definitely don't come with a snooze button.

You'll likely still be figuring out this whole parenting thing. Just when everyone's back to a full night's sleep, teeth begin to pop through. A look of dismay from someone whose opinion you normally couldn't care less about can send you into a tailspin, wondering if you're doing it "right".

The milestones will get you through the rough patches. Finding your baby talking happily to herself after naptime, seeing her sit up for the first time, getting a great big welcoming smile when you walk into the room — those are the times that reset your patience.

~Chapter 1~

Work It

Let's face it—all mom's work. But most people don't recognize what stay-at-home moms do as "work". They think that you must punch a timeclock or collect a corporate paycheck to be considered part of the workforce. Although that is quite an absurd assumption, we're going to define a "working mom" as one who collects an income for performing tasks outside of her duties at home. Of course that could be further broken down into many categories—distinguishing between those who work at home or in an office for example. For simplicity's sake, we'll group them together for now, and default to the standard title of "stay-at-home-mom" for all others.

When someone approaches me with the question, "Do you work or are you home with the kids?" I'd like to answer with a simple, "Yes." Then I'd like to explain that working and staying home with kids are not mutually exclusive. In fact, they most certainly co-exist. My kids are alive, dressed in clean clothes, and well fed, my office assignments are completed correctly and on time. Instead, I just explain my arrangement and give them my in-office schedule.

I doubt you'll find a mom who thinks that taking care of children, a home, and everything else that comes along with it is particularly easy—however enjoyable or satisfying it may be for them. Being responsible for the family and household's general well-being likely takes more patience, know-how, and time management than many projects that are assigned to even the best account managers.

If You Collected a Paycheck, It'd be a Big One

Those who have never tried it out for themselves often scoff at the research that suggests what a stay-at-home mom's salary would be if all of her tasks were broken down and charges were applied. Caregiver/babysitter, chef, chauffeur, social director, housekeeper, nurse, dry cleaner, accounts payable clerk . . . I'd venture a guess that any amount of money that is estimated is probably on the low end of the scale.

It goes without saying that, although some monetary compensation would be nice, moms don't do it for the money or the recognition. They do it for the hugs, for the satisfaction of knowing their children are well cared for. Income may be decreased drastically if the previously-employed woman's salary is sacrificed in order for her to stay home with her children. This may mean that you need to adapt to new budgets or habits. Even in households where circumstances easily allow for a mother (or father) to stay home, changes to your usual lifestyle may need to be made.

Those moms who are not able to stay home full time likely maintain a paying job for the benefit of their family, not just for fun. Their sacrifices are of a different nature. Even the most exciting jobs may pale in comparison to spending time with your kids. But just because a mom works does not mean that her children are neglected or that they don't spend time together.

The kids will appreciate you making the most of the time you do have together. That might mean that your chores are postponed until after their bedtime, leaving you with little time to wind down from your own day. Some days the dishes might just have to sit in the sink till tomorrow, the toys might stay scattered on the floor (they're going to get pulled out again tomorrow anyway). That's ok, quality time should take priority. As long as the house is clean enough to qualify as a healthy environment you don't need to stress over whether or not it's completely organized.

Jumping back into the job market—whether that means returning to your previous position after a brief maternity leave or starting a job search when your munchkins enroll in school—can prove quite challenging. Your frame of mind and vocabulary change in an alarmingly short amount of time. To you, speed to market no longer applies to how quickly you can prepare a product for public release, but instead how fast you can get to the grocery store and back before the babysitter leaves.

While your work ethic may remain strong, you'll likely find that your priorities and impression of importance may have shifted. Some women are eager to return to work, looking forward to the adult interaction and change of pace. Others may be completely preoccupied with thought and worries of what the baby is doing. If you're like me, it was a combination of the two (Type A personality, what can I say?). As I sat contemplating a marketing report my mind wandered to how many ounces the baby had taken at breakfast and if I was going to be able to pump enough to replenish that supply.

Work-at-Home Moms

Aside from the fact that stay-at-home moms work *at* home, some add the complexity of working *from* home. Having the ability to split your professional time between home and the office is a wonderful option, when available. You're able to maintain your professional status and income while spending time with your kids. It most certainly becomes a logistical challenge.

Your "lunch break" means taking the kids outside to run to prepare them for a good afternoon nap so that you can finish a project. You'll learn to type with one hand on a laptop that may as well be strapped to you since resting it on your lap would mean sitting down, and you know that doesn't happen very often. You'll carry on a conference call while breastfeeding — hoping no one hears your little monster slurping away.

No Country for New Moms

Ultimately, I'm left with one overarching question: Why is it seen as an indulgence or privilege to stay home with a new baby?! So many women are forced to return to work just weeks after giving birth — with a breast pump in her hand and a baby on her mind.

I love the United States and would not trade my citizenship for anything. However, if there was ever a time that I second guessed that statement, it was the first time I read about how poorly the benefits for mothers in the US are compared to other, often significantly less-developed, nations. The Federal Family and Medical Leave act stipulates that required employers (specific rules determine obligation) allow eligible employees (again, more rules) up to 12 weeks of unpaid leave within a 12 month period for birth of the employer's baby, for adoption procedures, to care for an immediate family member with a medical condition, or for medical leave when they are unable to work due to a serious health condition. Additionally, the employee has the right to return to the same (or an equivalent) position.

In addition to the Federal act, there are 11 states that have similar statutes. Some are better than others; California, Washington, and New Jersey offer partially-paid leave. Here's a look at how we stack up next to a few other countries:

Australia, the only other industrialized country in the world that does not offer paid leave to new mothers, is the closest in comparison but outdoes the US by protecting your job for a full year.

In Canada, new moms get up to 17 weeks of pregnancy leave and an additional 35 weeks of parental leave. Plus, dads can take up to 37 weeks off, either at another time or overlapping with the mother's leave!

German mothers enjoy a 14-week job-protected maternity leave, and collect 100 percent of their wages. After that time, paid leave is available to both parents until the child turns three.

Six to 10 weeks of prenatal leave and eight weeks of postnatal leave are paid at 60 percent in Japan.

Looks like what they say about doting Italian parents may just be true! After a five-month period of maternity leave paid at 80 percent, parents can take ten-month periods of leave, together or separately, at 30 percent of their earnings until the child's *eighth* birthday!

How do you feel about moving to France? France may offer the best support for parents, boasting a fully paid, job-protected, mandatory maternity leave starting six weeks before the baby's birth and extending to 10 weeks after. After that, either parent may be granted additional leave as needed up until the child's third birthday.

Sorry to get so technical on ya' — Details of eligibility and arguments over the level of involvement that the government should have are exhaustive. Although the number of children you have should not be determined by your income level, you need to take financial responsibility. Maternity leave and newborn care are just the beginning of a lifetime of liability. Daycare is another whole subject (sadly US citizens fare no better here).

~Chapter 2~

Did I Ask You? —
An Overabundance of Advice

By the time your baby hits the half year mark, you will undoubtedly have received more tips than you could possibly use, heard more stories than you could ever process. Parenting is possibly a subject on which you get more unsolicited advice than any other. Most of it is anecdotal, some of it is pushy, a small fraction of it is helpful.

It seems when you're the most exasperated someone tells you how their baby has slept at least eight hours through the night since the day they came home from the hospital. Before you breakdown in tears wondering if you're doing something wrong or if your baby was just born without the sleeping gene, remember that situations get idealized as they become memories.

It's part of what makes women want to have more children—forgetting the pain of labor, remembering the baby sleeping through the night within the first three weeks when it was really months before anyone in the house logged more than four straight hours of shut eye. Whether all these newfound storytellers are lying or just remember the "facts" a little differently than they actually happened, just know that a baby not sleeping is completely normal.

If their newborn did happen to sleep through the night immediately, or if their toddler skipped right over the terrible twos, you can take (vengeful) comfort in the fact that it will catch up with them. I know I'd rather deal with an infant who won't sleep than a teenager who will sleep with anyone who looks her way, or handle a rambunctious toddler rather than rebellious preteen.

There are new challenges at every turn. With each exciting developmental milestone comes a negative aspect. Try to focus on the positive—it's great that your son can finally talk—not on the negative that comes along with it—he can now yell no in response to your every request. Parents of older children will empathize, not judge—although they may laugh and gloat, happy that they're past that phase.

Regardless of the stage that you're in the midst of, comparing your child to other kids never does much good. Talk to your child's pediatrician if you detect a real problem or delay, but stressing over the fact that your friend's daughter is crawling and your son (who is two months older!) is content to sit and eat his feet is useless. Babies sleep when they want to, toddlers walk when they're ready, kids speak when the time is right.

~Chapter 3~

Multitasking Mama

Instead of worrying about the developmental progress of your child, focus on your proficiency as a parent. Just as we measure the motor skills of our children — dexterity with utensils, correct use of safety scissors, quickness at which she can do a puzzle — there is a standard against which we are evaluated as well.

Can you securely diaper a squirming baby (securely means the poop doesn't come out the leg holes)? Operate the bulb syringe (that's the mucus-sucker, for you newbies)? Fill and administer medicine from a vitamin dropper (extra points if baby doesn't gag)? Oh, and the test moderator looks nothing like the guy who read the instructions for the SATs; it's more likely that he'll be dressed in newborn-sized Carter's attire that you purchased.

After a few months of practice you might start to think you're pretty good at this. You can nurse the baby and type at a rate of 60 words per minute. You're working out four days a week (ish) and having sex nearly as often. Confidence and forward momentum are great, but don't get ahead of yourself. Before you know it teething will ruin your sleep training success, and the separation anxiety stage will make you late for work.

~Chapter 4~

No-Sleep / No-Sex Conspiracy

Sleepy Sleepy (you, not the baby)

You'd think that somewhere amidst the millions of years that women have been having babies that evolution would have taken care of babies knowing how to sleep. This is not the case. A binky haunted my dreams for years. The sound made by the little handle hitting the face plate as it fell out of my son's mouth onto the crib mattress was my notification that I would not be sleeping through the night.

I knew it was going to happen, I just didn't know when. While watching the last few minutes of a show (thank God for Tivo), during sex (Tivo for Sex still not perfected, working on pause feature), while drifting into blissful sleep (however short lived it would be) . . . from the moment of impact I had only a few minutes until I'd have to get up and give that binky back. We played that game until he was seven or eight months old and had developed the dexterity to get it back in his mouth. But it took me many more months to stop hearing the sound of phantom binkies falling in the night.

Some people would question why I went back in his room at all. Why not let him cry it out for a while? He'll eventually fall asleep without it, right? Just like childbirth methods and breastfeeding opinions, there are several approaches to teaching a baby how to sleep through the night. Co-sleeping, crying it out, rocking the baby to sleep, or putting him to bed while he's still awake . . . like so much else, there are so many choices, none of them necessarily right or wrong. But whichever you choose, someone will tell you you're doing it wrong.

You have to be comfortable with the method. You'll never know how long it will take your baby to fall asleep if you can't make it past four minutes without rushing into her room to soothe her. Crying it out refers to the baby but you may join in the tears. It's ok if you can't handle it and revert back to rocking her to sleep. Sometimes it's a matter of timing; you're ok with letting the baby cry but don't want to use that method when there's a toddler greatly in need of sleep in the next room.

While you do want to commit to a plan, you should also stay observant enough to recognize when something is not working. If persistent trying is not producing the results you want, try something new. Just be careful not to waver back and forth. Try to follow your instincts and not your emotions (easier said than done, I know). Babies like routines and can notice when you mess with theirs.

We took a hybrid approach the first time around. We tried to put the baby to bed when he was still somewhat awake but if he cried for too long (the time definition of "too long" changed often) we would go get him and help him back to sleep. Letting him cry would only lead to a hysterical, wide awake baby and increased arousals through the course of the night. My second son could be laid down without a tear. You're the parent but you may need to let your plan be partially dictated by your baby's personality.

Patience and endurance are compromised by exhaustion so you don't need to feel guilty if you give in. When my son's refusal to sleep in his crib coincided with my return to work, I would sometimes bring him into bed with us. We didn't "ruin" him; he now sleeps contently in his own bed (thankyouverymuch). It wasn't every night but it got us through. Sometimes on off nights, in my sleepless haze I would reach over and start patting and say, "Shh, it's ok," when I heard a cry, only to realize that the back I was patting belonged to my husband — the baby was still in his own room. But that's ok, it was the most contact I had had with my husband in months.

How Mommy Got Her Groove Back

Rekindling some romance and jumpstarting your sex life may take a little effort — some effort that you're not willing to give. You're all healed physically but you've fallen into a no-sex routine. Out of sight, out of mind; the less you have it, the less you want it. Although it's normal and completely understandable, it's a dangerous habit to fall into.

If you've taken a divide and conquer approach to life with a baby, you may just need to reconnect. Alternating tasks and tending to the baby can leave you running in opposite directions. If he washes dishes while you feed the baby, and you jump in the shower while he logs a little daddy time, the first time you really see each other may be when you collapse into bed. And by then, sleep seems much more appealing than sex.

Maybe you were anxious to have sex once you got the green light at your postpartum checkup but circumstances (read: crying babies) keep ruining your plans. When your intentions are good but execution is bad, the conspiracy theories begin to hatch. Everyone seems snug in their beds and you're just about to, ahem, get started, when a blood curdling scream fills the house. It's probably more of a teeth-cutting scream but no matter what you call it, it has poor timing. And that's one of the better scenarios. When the interruption comes when you're already in full swing you can be left wondering what to do. You don't want to stop but you know no one will be happy until that crying stops.

Whether the factors stopping you involve the fear of physical pain, not feeling in the mood, or are completely circumstantial, you need to deal with them. The timing will eventually work out so you need to work on the underlying issues that are keeping you from getting within reach of your partner. Talk to him about it. Even if you decide to forgo sex a little longer, keeping (or rebuilding) an intimate relationship is important.

~Chapter 5~

Getting Back in the Game

It's not just your relationship with your partner that is important. Your friendships may need a little maintenance as well, especially if you were too consumed with choosing nursery colors and recalculating your due date than returning phone calls and emails. Your friends who are fellow moms will understand and your non-mommy friends will gladly welcome you back. You'll be accepted with open arms, or more likely, baby- or shopping bag-filled arms. Either way, with plenty to catch up on, you won't have time to talk about who forgot to call whom back last time.

Doing Non-Mom Stuff

While you may not want, or be able, to rejoin the happy hour circuit, it's a good idea to spend some time with friends—without your baby. While play dates are a great way of amusing everyone, you'll need a little adult time. This can take the form of a quick lunch, decaf coffee and a pedicure, or more elaborate plans. It will depend on your schedule and level of comfort with leaving the baby. No matter where you end up, expect to have a moment of panic that you left the baby in the car before remembering she's safe at home with dad, grandmom, aunt, or other approved babysitter.

After a few minutes of the obligatory mommy chit-chat, put a moratorium on baby talk. Your grown-up time will feel like more of a break if it's not full of conversations regarding sleep schedules and the consistency of poop.

Flirting at the Playground—Mommy-friends

You'll have a whole new appreciation for your friends who had babies before you, and a whole new understanding of why they couldn't meet you for last minute drinks or take a spur of the moment road trip to the new outlet stores. If none of your friends have kids, you'll want to expand your circle.

You need a friend who's in a similar place, to whom you can confess. You don't have to feel guilty telling her that you're not *always* interested in your kids' games. She won't think you're married to a jerk when you complain that your husband never gets up in the middle of the night with the baby. She knows your house is clean even though it looks like a Cheerio graveyard under your couch—where cereal goes to die (or breed, it sometimes seems). When you tell her you don't feel like being a mom anymore she won't call Social Services because she'll understand that's just frustration and exhaustion talking and you love your kids more than anything. She won't even be jealous when your baby consistently sleeps through the night before hers. A friend like that is better than a therapist—and not nearly as costly.

If it's *new* mommy friends that you're seeking, you may be in a good place—if that place happens to be the park. You may find yourself trying to score some phone numbers for the first time in years. Your kids are similar ages, and hitting it off on the slides. She seems to be at least almost as cool of a mom as you. Now how do you get from, "That's a great stroller," to, "Do you want to get together some time?" If only you could gather up the moxie to ask. You'll suddenly have sympathy for all those guys you turned down in your single days. Go for it. Chances are she would appreciate the company of an adult too. Pretending not to be bored by games designed for an 18 month old is much easier to do while gossiping with your new friend about the other playground moms.

~Chapter 6~

A Day in the Life

By 8 am most moms have accomplished more than others will in all the remaining hours of the day combined. While most work shifts haven't yet begun, and many people are just getting their first cup of coffee, mom's already been on the job for hours. Babies don't have snooze buttons, and their internal clocks are never quite right.

Next time someone downplays the work involved with being a stay-at-home mom, or snidely says that it must be nice to get to work from home, share this Friday morning with them.

TGIF?

4:40am
Henry crying
Brayden calling for Daddy (who left for work about 5 minutes ago)

5:00am
Brayden finishing half a banana and a cup of water
Henry alternating fussing and tooting

5:30am
Brayden in bed reading books
Henry now crying, wants to nurse for 3rd time since 9pm

5:40am
Brayden, still in his diaper from overnight, yelling "PEE PEE!!" (guess I have to take him to the bathroom. After all, I started this potty training thing . . .)
Henry temporarily back in crib during pee pee run= not happy

6:00am
Brayden in bed playing with Prayer Bear (AKA loudest stuffed animal ever to exist—thanks G.G.)
Henry finally settling for water, falling back asleep despite said Bear

6:15am
"PEE PEE!!" (more came out—through the seat, onto the floor, my feet, and his pajama shorts)
Brayden, having been up for an hour and a half, is bored of being in bed, now just yelling
Henry, despite the noise, still asleep

6:30am
Brayden in my bed, watching and singing to Elmo (thank God for Tivo)

7:00am
Elmo's over
Brayden's sliding off the bed "Down! O-me-al [oatmeal]!"
Henry talking, yelling in crib

7:05am
My eyes are rejecting my contacts
Hit in face with poop smell as baby's bedroom door is opened
Brayden scaling crib rail to get in with Henry
Henry smiling (poop in diaper and on sheets)

7:15am
Henry, crib, and changing table, changed
Brayden peeing (apparently takes after me)
Poop laundry started

7:45am
Brayden finishing 2nd half of banana and 2 packs of oatmeal
Henry inhaling "gourmet" Banana Orange Medley and rice cereal (mmm, mmm)
Sending my first work email of the day

8:00am
Little Einsteins coming on (aahhh)
Stale cake for breakfast

Forecast:
Desired—Play nicely all morning, eat lunch, synchronize naps
Probable—Toys being thrown by mid-morning, too tired to eat lunch, alternating naps

Although a testimony like that doesn't make it abundantly clear, even amid the chaos of life you'll realize how wonderful it is. You can't give away the bad moments without losing the good ones.

Take it one day at a time. When you're in the middle of a particularly difficult day remind yourself that you got through the previous day and you'll get through this one too.

Not all days are bad. In fact, many of them are really, really good. Getting into a routine — not a strict schedule, but a general timeline of events — is very helpful. Children like structure. Maintaining a routine does not mean that you can never spend a day away from home, or break the schedule. Build flexibility into your day whenever possible, although consistency is key. Keep naptime at roughly the same time each day and your child will learn to expect it. He may not always be excited to stop playing and go lay down, but you'll likely find that the times he falls asleep within five minutes greatly outnumber the times he screams for twenty minutes until you agree to let him come downstairs and watch a show if he promises to stay on the sofa quietly (quite a gamble on your part).

Losing, Then Quickly Regaining, Your Adult Identity

Spending all day every day with your child(ren) may make you forget your grown-up identity. Remember to spend some time with adults and turn on the news or sign up for pop culture emails so that you stay in touch with reality.

Here are some signs that you're drifting away:

- Labor Day has a whole new meaning to you
- The Elmo potty song has been stuck in your head for the past eight days but you can't name a song released in the last six months.
- You find yourself fantasizing about one of the guys from Disney's Imagination Movers. (If the object of your fantasy is animated you're even farther gone!)
- You define "dressed up" as wearing wedge flip flops instead of your normal flat ones.
- You watched the rest of that G-rated movie after your daughter fell asleep . . . because you were curious how it was going to end.
- You and your partner call each other Mommy or Daddy when not in the presence of your kids. (This is excused if it's during the first month of being a new parent as the novelty has not yet worn off.)
- You have begun taking sippy cups of coffee in the car instead of travel mugs.

- The last novel you read was during the sleepless nights of your last trimester.
- You own only nursing bras although you weaned the baby two months ago.
- Your email address includes the word "mommy".

If they seem all too familiar to you, try subscribing to a magazine that doesn't relate to parenting. Hollywood gossip, or fashion and beauty, magazines can be a cheap thrill. Try staying up late. You haven't pulled as many all nighters as you have lately since sophomore year of college and you're still surviving. One more night isn't going to make a difference. Staying up to watch the late show can make you feel like an adult again.

~Chapter 7~

Starting Over

Don't be surprised when, while you're addressing invitations to your baby's first birthday party, you burst into tears. When I was packing up clothes that the baby had grown out of, and my husband said, "Give it away or throw it away. We won't be using it again," I had a similar reaction. Even if you complained for the first 364 days of his life, you'll be sad when your baby turns one.

The idea of starting the process all over again may send you running. Even if you conceived easily, had a great pregnancy, and have adjusted quite nicely to life with baby, beginning again can sound like a daunting task. How long will it take this time? Will your body bounce back as well after a second pregnancy? Can your relationship handle it? You and your partner — yes, he should definitely be involved in the decision making process — have a tough decision ahead of you.

If you make the decision to have another baby, you may wonder if you'll love the next one as much as you love your first. That's another amazing thing about motherhood, the ever-expanding supply of love. Although getting through all the learning stages with your first baby may have led to an amazing bond, you'll connect with your second baby (and each subsequent baby after that) over something else.

Cultivating a unique relationship with your second baby may be even easier if she is the opposite sex as your first. The mommy's boy connection can be very different than the mother-daughter dynamic. Some say that babies bond more easily with the parent of the opposite sex, but I believe that, like so many other things, it all depends on the kid. You'll undoubtedly alternate between being the good parent and the bad — sometimes on a daily case-by-case basis, sometimes over several years (the teenage ones). But no matter their opinion of you, you'll still think that you have the best child(ren) that God ever created.

Closing

Motherhood is the meaning of life, quite literally. It is what I was meant to do. That being said, it doesn't mean I'll become one of those crazy ladies who births 17 kids in 18 years (personal opinion, sorry).

I'm guilty of so many of the offenses that are listed within the pages of this book. Although I gave a little grace period, I always asked newlyweds when they thought they'd have a baby until a few kinks in our plan delayed my pregnancy by a year or so. I admit that I thought I was *the* better parent a time or two when compared to my husband, and *a* better parent when compared to other moms. A few (countless) mistakes quickly knocked me from my pedestal. I never understood why a friend couldn't keep her kid quiet during our ten minute phone conversation until I had my own little talkative tot.

I have learned a lot but I have a sneaking suspicion that it's only a fraction of what I have left to find out. If you have gained anything from my insight — even if it was what *not* to do — I'm glad.

I hope you have fun making a baby — no matter how long it takes.
I hope you are able to realize the beauty of pregnancy — not just see the stretch marks.
I hope that being a parent means the world to you and that you cherish your children — even when they're throwing rice at each other.

Daddy Dictionary (annotated edition)

Baby Brain — your partner was probably always the smarter one between the two of you, right? Being overwhelmed, receiving a plethora of new information, and hormones can change that. This can range from stumbling over a word here and there to being an all out airhead about anything not baby-related. It may be the worst when she's breastfeeding, as the baby literally sucks the intelligence out of her. Flare ups can continue long after your kids go to college though. Never, ever, point this out to your partner, or even agree if she mentions it.

Burp the Baby — this is not a request to belch the baby's name. Instead, pat or rub your baby's back gently but firmly while he's in an upright position. Depending on the size, age, and stability level of your baby, this works best with you holding him belly to chest with you so that his head is at your shoulder, or sitting on your lap. Stand by for spit up.

Cereal — around six months of age your baby can eat cereal. Don't worry, you don't have to share your Lucky Charms. Baby cereal consists of tiny flakes that mix into a cream of wheat type substance when you add water.

Changing a Diaper — let's compare this to something you know, like changing a tire. You don't want to remove the old one until you know you have a spare. Same rule applies here; get a clean diaper out before you begin. As you'd remove the lug nuts that hold the tire on the wheel, here you should remove the sticky tabs that hold the diaper on the baby. You may leave the diaper under the baby while you wipe up excess debris, just as resting the tire under the car is a good idea. Align the new diaper under the baby and secure it back in place by pulling the sticky tabs from the back around to the front, just as you'd tighten the lug nuts once the new tire is back on.

Quickening — the old school way to say the baby is moving in utero, sometimes called kicking. (Do not attempt to reenact the belly-bursting scene from Alien.) Can also refer to the accelerated pace at which your pregnant partner now walks to the bathroom.

Soft Spot — clinically called the anterior fontanel, this is, as the name suggests, a soft spot in your baby's skull. Found on the top of your baby's head, this is one of six of these spots that actually made your baby's head flexible enough to fit through the birth canal. This term may also relate to the newly-mushy place in your heart for your baby.

Umbilical cord — it's the squiggly thing that kinda' looks like a bungee cord attached to your baby's bellybutton. It's actually your baby's life source during his time in utero. This is what people are talking about when they ask if you're going to cut the cord.

Weight Gain — an important part of pregnancy — for your pregnant partner. It is not necessary, or justifiable, for *you* to gain weight unless *you* plan on delivering the baby via *your* genitals. While it is often exciting for an expectant mom to start showing, comments that include such terms as *filling out, packin' on the pounds,* or *size of a house* will not be taken graciously.

Disclaimer ~ Keeping it PC

Of course I recognize that all dads aren't idiots. Some fathers are very well-read on the topics of pregnancy, delivery, and childcare; some are just naturals; most learn as they go!

The dumbed-down language found here, and throughout the book, is intended to educate. It was used to illustrate a point, and occasionally for the sake of humor (and maybe a gratuitous laugh or two).

True Confessions

Pregnancy and parenting can lead to some pretty great stories. While some are unique to each individual experience, others transcend all boundaries and become universally true.

The Front Nine

Enough with the sticks! The second a woman becomes pregnant, her big toe should turn blue. It would make life so much easier!

~Tracey

My husband went with me to my very first trip to the OB-GYN to confirm my first pregnancy. We were both so very excited. We thought nothing of it when the doctor told us they were going to do an ultrasound . . . until I found out exactly *how* they do an ultrasound when you're just a few weeks pregnant. Just how is it that my girlfriends failed to warn me about the *internal* ultrasound?! EW!!

~Tracey from the burbs

So I go to the store to pick up some stuff and on my list is Shampoo and Conditioner. I like to change up the brands and flavors each time I go so I was looking for something new. I end up walking out with two bottles of Conditioner, one big, one small — enough Conditioner to last a year. So a few days later when we are really, *really* out of shampoo, I venture back to the store to fix my previous wrong. I go in with 3 things on my list: Shampoo, deodorant for my husband, and Tums (a *big* bottle of Tums). I walk out with deodorant for my husband, body lotion for myself, a box of gourmet mint M&M's, and a squirrel squeaky toy for my dog. Oh yeah . . . and another bottle of Conditioner. I of course also forgot the Tums. Oh, Baby brain!

~Jacqui — expectant mother of #1, T minus 23 weeks

My favorite parts of pregnancy:
- Compliments on how cute I looked
- Extra help from strangers
- Watching my belly ripple around from baby movements after dinner
- Hearing the baby's heartbeat at doctor visits

~Kristin — mom of 2 boys, ages 8 months and 3 years

I saw that when I was noticeably pregnant but not wearing my wedding ring, people gave me dirty (or at least questionable) looks. Apparently many people still have to work on their quick judgments.

>~Married with 2 babies (and sometimes swollen fingers)

Labor of Love

Lesson learned: Sex induces labor.

>~Kristin—mom of 2 boys, ages 8 months and 3 years

No doubt that bringing another human being, namely a baby, into this world is nothing short of a miracle!! Many things must be aligned for Conception to occur, Pregnancy to prevail and Childbirth to happen. But what amazes me most, is how that small creature depends solely on you for 9 months in utero, and often long after. When you first see and hold your newborn, you feel an overwhelming sense of responsibility knowing that you will protect this child as no other being in your life, and will sacrifice everything to make her life as perfect as possible. That child is truly your pride and joy.

>~jba3xmom

Delivery Surprises:
- Being able to remember every moment of Shane's delivery and not much of Brett's.
- Feeling a closeness to my husband that had never before been experienced.

>~Kristin—mom of 2 boys, ages 8 months and 3 years

Thank God for that Mommy chemical that makes you forget the pain.

>~Jacqui—expectant mother of #1, T minus 23 weeks

Neither of my babies would stay in the nursery at the hospital when they were born—they cried for Mommy! The nurse came walking into my room and said, "They won't stop crying, they want their mommy!" Of course, I had no sleep in the hospital, but loved the fact that my babies wanted *me* instead of the nursery!

>~Jeannie—mom of 2 girls, now 19 and 21

Adventures in Breastfeeding

I had not purchased a breast pump before Shane was born, just in case breastfeeding did not work for me. At home, 3 days after Shane was born, my breasts were so engorged and my milk let down as I was stepping out of the shower. Drip, drip, drip, drip, drip. I called for some help from Dave and he ran over with 2 dixie cups. I went out and purchased a breast pump.

~Kristin — mom of 2 boys, ages 8 months and 3 years

My sister and her husband went to a work Christmas Party and their daughter, who was only a few months old, was nursing at the time. We minded her and she wouldn't stop crying so my husband asked me to try to nurse her to get her to stop since I was also nursing my own daughter at the time. Well if you could have seen her face when I put my boob in her mouth — POISON! It felt weird for me too and needless to say that was the end of that!

~Jeannie — mom of 2 girls, now 19 and 21

Life with Baby

As a new mom, I learned to prioritize everything I do, including my showers. Face and body first, shampoo and conditioner, and then, if she's still sleeping, I might even have enough time to shave my legs!

~Hairy Legs in Willow Grove, PA

While I put my makeup on, I would lay Jill on the bathroom floor on her back and she would just flap her arms and make big eyes. Well, when she would start crying and I couldn't get her to stop, I would take her into the bathroom and lay her on the floor and she would stop crying; it was the craziest thing! Was it comfort? the lights? Who knows but it worked!

~Jeannie — mom of 2 girls, now 19 and 21

One day, our brand new baby boy was sitting pleasantly in the infant swing in the living room while our toddler played nearby. I went into the kitchen (less than 20 feet away) for a moment or two to take care of something when I heard the baby begin to cry. I quickly returned to the living room to find the infant on the floor and the toddler sitting in the swing.

~Tracey from the burbs

When Tyler was 2 weeks old, I got brave enough to venture to church with he and Abby (3 ½) in matching outfits. I was even a few minutes early . . . I was so proud of myself! I was clean, hair done and a little make-up! So glad to be going it alone with *two* kids. All was going great, Tyler peacefully asleep in my arms and Abby looking angelic kissing him on the head every once in a while. It came time for Communion and I stood up, baby still sleeping and Abby following behind. I was so "together" and in control . . . I headed up the aisle and turned around to check that Abby was following. I glanced back in time to see her LICKING the pews on her way by each one . . . during flu season no less!! It was at that time that I realized I was never again going to be fully in control. (I have learned since then that control is overrated.) I chose instead to giggle at myself, the situation, and the fact that for years to come I would laugh about that moment!

~Joanie — mother of 2, ages 11 and 7

Our little boy was 20 months old when we welcomed our second little guy into the world. All the stories I'd heard about jealousy and scrambling for mommy's attention were right on target. Needless to say, the first month or so was truly a test of wills, patience and unconditional love. One sunny morning, the three of us were hanging out in the living room. I had the door open to the deck so we could enjoy some fresh air and sunshine. My toddler was wandering in and out between the living room and the deck while my infant was playing on his activity mat on the living room floor. Things seemed under control and in harmony, so I thought I could steal a few minutes to run upstairs. A minute or so later, when I was in the bathroom, I heard the baby start to cry. I scrambled to get back downstairs as quickly as possible. When I got to the bottom of the steps, I found my toddler sprinkling handfuls of dirt from my potted plants onto the baby. It was though the jealousy had finally reached its peak and he was trying to bury the baby alive!

~Tracey from the burbs

After many years of doing daycare, I had a family I became very close with. We really bonded and were good friends. Their middle child, Jake, was the youngest baby I ever took care of. He started at my home at 3 months and stayed with me until he was 9 years old. Jake was a bully, pure and simple. Anything or anyone that he could control to his benefit made him quite happy. One day, after many attempts to divert his actions to positive play, he really became hyper. He started running through the house, throwing, hitting, yelling, and teasing everyone. I just lost it and started chasing him. I almost had him by the collar when he turned, stopped dead in his tracks, put up his fists, looked me straight in the eye, and said, "Bring it on Babysitter!!" Well I was shocked to say the least and just started laughing and so did Jake. By the way, Jake is now 15 and every time we see each other we talk about that day!

~Barbara — Mother of 2, Grandmother of 5,
Daycare Provider — 34 years to many, many children

I had my "woman visit" and I took all 4 boys to the appointment thinking that it was a normal visit. She asked me to change into a gown and boy was I surprised. I told the older boys to stand near my head and began talking to Barbara. Next thing I knew Tanner was down at the stirrups (2 years old) asking "What is she doing and what is that inside you?" Well I think he might be an OB-GYN.

~Dana — mom of half a dozen

As part of my annual review, I had to fill out a self-evaluation. There's a section asking for "Examples of Major Achievements during Review Period". I was very tempted to write "Completing all work on time while juggling a toddler who's quickly approaching terrible two's and a 20 pound – 6 month old who nurses every three hours like clockwork"!

~Work-at-home-mom

Desperate Times Call for Desperate Measures

re: Potty Training
When they have to go they have to go. Don't be surprised when you're driving down the Turnpike and your child says he has to pee. You're miles from the next rest stop and who knows how long they can wait. I've pulled over on most area highways for Evan (NJ Turnpike, PA Turnpike, I-95, and many parking lots) so he could leave his puddle or wash the car tire. I had him climb to the front passenger seat and then have him stand on the side rails and pee out. Pooping was even funnier. We were at a party store and Evan needed to poop. The store of course was not one I would expect to have a sanitary bathroom and of course the employees said they did not have one. So I took a plastic bag from the store, had him sit over one of my legs in the parking lot, and poop into the bag. Of course most times he has to poop the pee comes with it, but we managed to get it all in the bag and stay dry!!

~Carmela – mom of 2 boys

One afternoon, my sister Brooke and I took her car to run a quick errand with one of my sons. Since we wouldn't be gone long, I left the house without the diaper bag. So when he pooped all over the place, we had only the contents of her gym bag that was in the trunk to use! I laid the towel inside the trunk as a changing pad and used her water bottle to wet a sock to wipe him. I put the other sock on his penis and wrapped a t-shirt around him for double protection for the ride home!

~Dana – mom of half a dozen

Daddy Knows Best

When my son was an infant, he often "pooped out" of his diaper. This called for lots of outfit changes, and lots of rinsing and soaking. After one particular episode, I walked into our laundry room to find my husband using a paint stirrer to swirl poopy clothes in a bucket in an attempt to get the poop off without having to touch it!

~wife of McGuyver-wannabe

Dawn had been babysitting Shane and I left her some frozen milk. She took Shane out to the mall with the kids. Mike came home and was re-heating some cinnamon buns. He looked in the freezer and to his surprise saw what he thought was extra icing for the top of his buns. Just as he was about to thaw it out, Dawn walked in and stopped him and announced, "What are you doing? That is Kris's breast milk."

~Kristin — mom of 2 boys, ages 8 months and 3 years

From the Mouths of Babies

One morning Evie got up from the kitchen table and ran all the way around the island to the sink to have her face wiped off. I said, "Evie, you ran around in a circle." She said, "No mom, I run in a rectangle! See?" And then she ran around the island again emphasizing the corners.

~Denise

I was up late with Little Larry (teething, etc), and around 5a.m. I opened a new bottle of Tylenol and gave him his dose. Being half asleep I must not have closed the *child proof* lid all the way. Ashley was about 33 months, and when she woke up she went downstairs first. By the time I came downstairs she was coming out of the bathroom with the empty — yes empty — bottle of Tylenol in her hand saying, "Mommy this was dewicious!" I knew it was a full bottle so the first thing I did was call Poison Control. The woman was great. She calmly asked if I had syrup of ipecac. I did but was not really sure where I hid it to keep it out of the kids' reach . . . ironic that I didn't do that with a full bottle of Tylenol!!

She said, "I will give you exactly five minutes to locate it, otherwise take a spoon and your child to the drugstore, buy some and give it to her at the store." I found it, gave it to her, and she threw up all the Tylenol. It took her about six throw ups but it all came out. Poison Control called me all throughout the day to see how she was doing and then called the next day. I asked the woman, after thanking her a million times, what would have happened. She said she would have fallen asleep and her liver would have shut down and by the time I thought her nap was over . . . well . . . you know what. Scary, huh?! Thank goodness she told me, "MOMMY THIS WAS DEWICIOUS!" We say it all the time till this day!

~Kathy with the red/brown/short/
long/curly/straight hair, 9 siblings, mom of 4

I was changing my newborn son's diaper when my 3 year old daughter walked in and said, "Mommy, What's that?" (pointing to his penis). "I WANT ONE OF THEM!!!!" I couldn't help but smile and whisper under my breath, "Someday honey, someday."

~Terry — mom of 5

Realizations

I'd like to think that just like scratches on my hardwood floors, stretch marks give my belly character!

~Learning to Love It Anyway, mom of 2

Play-Doh and potty training are best done outdoors.

~Kristin — mom of 2 boys, ages 8 months and 3 years

I used to think that the most beautiful thing was that untouched blanket of white that you see out the window the morning after a heavy snow. Now that I'm a mom, I've come to realize that the disruption of that same snow by toddler size 6 footprints makes it an even more amazing view. (The same goes for footprints in the sand or on the bathmat.)

~Kelly — mom of 2 boys, ages 9 months and 2 years

Just when you think you think you have it together, a toddler reminds you who's really in charge.

~Clueless Mama

The greatest thing you can give your children is a great marriage, love, and consistency. Children are little sponges and they watch everything, and *they* are one day going to be a husband or wife. They are learning from us how to be that person, how to be men and women. And don't we need some great men these days?! Men for our daughters to marry.

~Dana — mom of 5 little men, and 1 little lady

When expecting my second child, I wondered if I could split my love for my daughter (with a new baby), and soon realized that I had enough love for him, too. In fact, I had a third child, and love each one of them differently than the other, no more, no less. Of the achievements I have made in my life, birthing three children has been my greatest. And I could not have done it without the support of my best friend, my husband.

~jba3xmom

Acknowledgements

I want to thank my Mom for being such a great example of what a mother should be. You have been an editor in my life, and now in my work as well.

Thanks to Tracey, my best friend and English expert, for being honest with me about this book just as you are with everything.

And Kristin, someone who understands the words on these pages all too well—You are my rainy day rescuer, and my cherished friend.

Thanks to Sarah for making my words pretty. You often *can* judge a book by its cover, and you made this one worthy!

My deep appreciation goes to Xlibris who helped me realize my dreams by making me a published author.